Lernkrimi Englisch

Die Jagd nach dem Vampir

Story: Marc Hillefeld
Übersetzung: Sarah Nowotny

Compact Verlag

Bisher sind in dieser Reihe erschienen:

- Compact Lernkrimi Englisch Grammatik
- Compact Lernkrimi Englisch Konversation
- Compact Lernkrimi Englisch Grundwortschatz
- Compact Lernkrimi Englisch Aufbauwortschatz

Weitere Titel sind in Vorbereitung.

Chefredaktion: Ilse Hell
Redaktion: Julia Kotzschmar
Redaktionsassistenz: Florian Markgraf
Fachredaktion: Linda Wright
Produktion: Henning Liebke
Typografischer Entwurf: Maria Seidel
Umschlaggestaltung: Carsten Abelbeck
Titelillustration: Karl Knospe
ISBN: 3-8174-7305-2
7273051

Besuchen Sie uns im Internet: www.compactverlag.de

Vorwort

Mit dem neuen, spannenden Compact Lernkrimi können Sie Ihre Englischkenntnisse auf schnelle und einfache Weise vertiefen, auffrischen und überprüfen.
Inspector Hudson erleichtert das Sprachtraining mit Action und Humor. Er und seine mysteriösen Kriminalfälle stehen im Mittelpunkt einer zusammenhängenden Story.
Der Krimi wird auf jeder Seite durch abwechslungsreiche und kurzweilige Übungen ergänzt, die das Lernen unterhaltsam und spannend machen.
Prüfen Sie Ihr Englisch in Lückentexten, Zuordnungs- und Übersetzungsaufgaben, in Buchstabenspielen und Kreuzworträtseln!
Ob im Bus oder in der Bahn, im Wartezimmer, zu Hause oder in der Mittagspause – das Sprachtraining im handlichen Format bietet die ideale Trainingsmöglichkeit für zwischendurch.
Schreiben Sie die Lösungen einfach ins Buch!
Die richtigen Antworten sind in einem eigenen Lösungsteil zusammengefasst.

Und nun kann die Spannung beginnen …

Viel Spaß und Erfolg!

Inhalt

Story

James Hudson arbeitet als Inspector bei der legendären Polizeibehörde Scotland Yard. Er ist einer der fähigsten Männer und wird immer dann zu Rate gezogen, wenn seine Kollegen mal wieder vor einem Rätsel stehen. Seine resolute und krimibegeisterte Haushälterin Miss Paddington unterstützt ihn stets mit liebevoller Fürsorge. Und insgeheim verfolgt sie noch ein weiteres Ziel: ihn endlich mit der jungen, attraktiven Versicherungsagentin Elvira Elliot zu verkuppeln.

In London treibt ein mysteriöser Verbrecher sein Unwesen. Leichenblass und mit wehendem Mantel versetzt er die Menschen in Angst und Schrecken.
Hudson und Miss Paddington folgen der rätselhaften Erscheinung durch die Nacht ...
Ist ein längst vergessener Mythos zum Leben erwacht? Gibt es eine Verbindung zu den Londoner Filmstudios? Werden Hudson und Miss Paddington der geheimnisvollen Gruft entkommen?
Nach und nach gelingt es Inspector Hudson, Licht in das Dunkel des Unerklärlichen zu bringen ...

The Hunt for the Vampire

Michael Carlyle was more nervous than he had ever been before in his life. With shaking hands he held the rose that he had just bought from a street seller.
There was a perfect full moon above the park which gave the trees a silvery light.
A light ground fog made the whole park look like a beautiful, romantic painting.
Michael looked at his watch again; for the hundredth time that evening.
Five minutes to midnight.

Übung 1: Finden Sie das passende Gegenteil und setzen Sie die richtige Ziffer ein!

1. midnight	9	dirty
2. light	5	ugly
3. big	7	morning
4. tall	10	sad
5. beautiful		heavy
6. dark		thin
7. evening		light
8. thick	1	midday
9. clean		short
10. happy	3	small

Liza was due to finish work about now. He had met her two weeks ago in the smoky student pub where she worked as a waitress to finance her studies.

For a whole week he had gone to the pub every evening to see Liza again, although he had exams at the university soon and didn't really have the time to go to the pub in the evening.

Or the money, for that matter.

After a couple of days – he had had to borrow some money from his flatmate – Michael had finally found the courage to speak to Liza. Her smile had charmed him right from the beginning. And, to his great surprise and joy, she had agreed to go out with him.

ÜBUNG 2 !

Übung 2: Welche Übersetzung stimmt?

1. Kannst du mir etwas Geld leihen?
   - a) ☐ Can you borrow me some money?
   - b) ☐ Can you lend me some money?

2. Sie hat ein nettes Lächeln.
   - a) ☐ She has a nice smile.
   - b) ☐ She has a nice laugh.

3. Ich habe heute Nachmittag einen Termin beim Zahnarzt.
   - a) ☐ I have an appointment at the dentist's this afternoon.
   - b) ☐ I have a date with the dentist this afternoon.

4. Michael bekam eine Überraschung.
   - a) ☐ Michael became a surprise.
   - b) ☐ Michael got a surprise.

This evening was their first date. They were going to meet at midnight under the old clock in the city park. Michael looked around. The ground fog was thicker, but there were no other people for miles around.

Übung 3: Lesen Sie den Text weiter und setzen Sie die Substantive in Klammern richtig ein!
(air, fog, hands, man, moonlight, night, park, pub, rose, walk)

Suddenly a shadowy figure came out of the 1. *fog*. Michael jumped – he couldn't stop himself.

Could it be – yes, it was Liza. She came towards the young 2. ________, smiling.

"There you are," she called. "I was afraid that I wouldn't find you in the fog."

"H-Hello," stammered Michael. He found it difficult to speak. Instead he held out the 3. ________ to her. His 4. ________ were shaking, and not only because of the cold, wet 5. ________.

"Oh, that's very kind of you," smiled Liza.

Here in the 6. ________ she looked even more beautiful than in the dark 7. ________.

"I, uhhm, would you like to go for a little 8. ________?" asked Michael, shyly.

"Why not? It's such a wonderful moonlit 9.________. And we're all alone here in the 10. ________."

Michael Carlyle could not believe his luck. Liza put her arm through his. She was now near enough for him to smell her perfume. And the cold smoke from the pub where she worked. But he didn't mind that at all. Michael was just thinking how perfect the evening was, when the horror struck.

At first it was only a dark shadow that rose from the silvery fog. Michael and Liza jumped. A tall figure appeared. The man was wearing a long, black coat that almost looked like a cape. His face was very white and shone in the moonlight. He didn't say a word, but simply stood there and stared at Michael and Liza.

! ÜBUNG 4

Übung 4: Welche Farbe ist gemeint?

1. The man's face was as __________ as snow.
2. Vampires love to drink fresh, __________ blood.
3. His coat was dark; as __________ as night.
4. When it rains a lot, the grass is very __________.
5. When it doesn't rain for a long time, the grass is __________.
6. My grandfather is 70 years old and his hair is __________.
7. There were some nice __________ bananas in the kitchen.
8. The sun shone brightly on the deep __________ sea.
9. __________ is a colour and it is also a type of fruit.

"C-Can I help you?" asked Michael, standing protectively in front of Liza.
The man did not answer.
Instead he raised his arms so that his coat fluttered like a pair of

black wings. Very slowly, a grin spread across the white face. "Yes …, you can help me," said the mysterious man in an icy voice, which seemed to come from far away. "I'm hungry … very hungry."

Liza pointed over her shoulder with her thumb.

"Er, o-over there, at the other end of the park, there's a Salvation Army soup kitchen. I'm sure you will –"

Liza stopped speaking in the middle of the sentence as the stranger's lips opened further.

A pair of long, shiny fangs could be seen.

"I'm hungry," said the man, staring at Liza's neck. "For your … blood!"

Michael and Liza both screamed, then turned and ran. All they wanted was to get away from here.

They ran through the park towards the distant exit as if they had lost their senses.

But the man did not follow them. He simply let his cape flutter in the wind and laughed.

Then he turned and disappeared back into the shadows. His laughter echoed for a long time through the dark park.

Übung 5: Welche Wörter gehören zusammen?
Setzen Sie die richtigen Ziffern ein!

1.	fish and	☐	day
2.	bread and	☐	play
3.	salt and	☐	wife
4.	night and	☐	vegetables
5.	black and	☐	chips
6.	up and	☐	daughter
7.	brush and	☐	butter

8. husband and	☐	down
9. brother and	☐	white
10. son and	☐	pepper
11. work and	☐	comb
12. fruit and	☐	sister
13. sun and	☐	winter
14. summer and	☐	rain
15. now and	☐	again

The air on this sunny Saturday morning was filled with the shouts of the street sellers and the delicious scent of fish and chips.
Inspector James Hudson and Elvira Elliot were walking slowly through Camden Market, one of the most famous of London's flea markets.
The hustle and bustle was exciting. There were lots of little stalls standing very close together, and the sellers were shouting in praise of their goods. Kitsch and junk, old clothes, antiques, handicrafts and organic food – you could find anything and everything at Camden Market.
However, James Hudson and Elvira were not here for pleasure. Due to a strange new case that the inspector was working on, they had spent the last few weekends walking through London's flea markets.

ÜBUNG 6 !

Übung 6: Ordnen Sie die Buchstaben zu sinnvollen Wörtern!

Elvira stopped at a stall selling old (1. tcohlse) *clothes* from the 1970s.

The (2. pteronsic) ____________________ rolled his eyes.

"Ooh," said Elvira, holding up a (3. arip) ________________ of bright orange (4. sosrutre) ________________.

"Look, James, aren't these trousers great?"

"Mmmm," muttered Hudson, "they are if you want to get a job as a (5. daor krerow) ________________ ________________ on the motorway. All you need now is a luminous (6. tsacoawit) ________________ to go with them."

Elvira laughed and shook her (7. edha) ________________.

"Oh, James, you don't know anything about (8. snafiho) ________________. Clothes from the 70s are still really trendy."

Then the young insurance agent turned to the seller, a pale student, whose eyes lit up at the thought of making some money.
"Only £12, Miss," he said. "It's a bargain! You won't find another authentic pair of trousers like these so easily."
"No," murmured Hudson to himself, "not unless you look at the next stall."
Hudson looked around. He had the impression that most of the market stalls were selling 1970s clothes. Personally, he was glad that that time and its fashion were in the past.
Elvira smiled and looked at Hudson playfully.
"What did you wear in the 1970s, James?"
"I had at least one pair of carrot-coloured trousers, I know that much for sure."
Elvira laughed again and put the orange trousers back.

Übung 7: Übersetzen Sie und enträtseln Sie das Lösungswort!

1. Mütze □ _ _
2. Hausschuhe _ □ _ _ _ _ _ _
3. Hose _ _ □ _ _ _ _ _
4. Rock _ _ _ _ □
5. kurze Hose _ □ _ _ _ _
6. Kleid _ _ □ _ _
7. Hemd □ _ _ _ _

Lösung: _ _ _ _ _ _ _

“Sorry,” she said to the salesman. “But my charming friend doesn’t seem to like them.”
The light went out of the student’s eyes.
“What a pity. But what about this?”
The young man reached into a box behind his stand and pulled out a ridiculously large cap made of checked material.
Hudson opened his eyes wide.
“For goodness’ sake!” he exclaimed.
Elvira smiled at the salesman and shook her head.
“Thank you. I’ll pass it. I don’t think our inspector here is in the mood for shopping today.”
The young man behind the stall looked shocked.
“I-Inspector?” he stammered.
It was clear that he had not come by all of the goods he was selling completely legally.
But today, at least, he didn’t need to worry. Inspector James

Hudson was at the flea market because of a completely different case. And it was time to remind Elvira Elliot of this fact.
"Please don't forget why we're here, Elvira," said Hudson, pleasantly. "The case that I've asked you to help me with is extremely sensitive. The tourist board is going crazy and wants us to catch these criminals as quickly as possible, before even more tourists become frightened and stay at home."
Elvira Elliot sighed.
"All right, James, I'm coming."

Übung 8: Welches Wort ist das „schwarze Schaf"?

1. frightened, afraid, scared, tired ______
2. surprised, shocked, amazed, astonished ______
3. like, enjoy, hate, love ______
4. driver, tourist, holidaymaker, traveller ______
5. robber, policeman, thief, murderer ______
6. bank, supermarket, butcher's, baker's ______
7. beautiful, attractive, busy, pretty ______
8. happy, angry, glad, pleased ______
9. glass, knife, fork, spoon ______

Elvira put her arm through Hudson's, and they continued on their way through the flea market.
"If you don't look a bit more relaxed, James, no-one will believe that we are tourists from the English provinces," smiled Elvira.

"You look so serious that everyone can see you're a policeman – you might as well have put on your uniform."
"I don't wear a uniform, Elvira," answered James Hudson, smiling back at her. "And I'll try to look more pleasant from now on. I just don't find it easy to stop thinking like a policeman. Look around you …"

Übung 9: Unterstreichen Sie die Namen der Gegenstände, die man im Büro finden könnte!

The inspector pointed to the many stalls in Camden Market. They seemed to be sinking under the weight of all the old clothes, CDs and old records, televisions and stereo systems, furniture and antiques, lamps and cutlery. Some were selling complete computer systems, and one seller had lots of different fax machines and other office equipment. At the end of the market there was a long row of bicycles shining in the morning sun. The stall next to them was even selling car radios and car tyres.

Hudson shook his head.
"I wouldn't like to know where all of these things have come from. I bet half of all the articles here were stolen. It looks exactly like the room in Scotland Yard where we keep all the stolen goods that we find."
Elvira laughed and put her arm around Inspector Hudsons's shoulders.
"Don't be so negative, James. Besides, I don't believe that all of these things are stolen goods. When I was a student, I often sold stuff at flea markets. The whole business is a cycle: you buy some junk at the flea market, are really enthusiastic about it – and

then you realise that you don't need it after all and sell it again."
"And if you can, you make a profit, eh?" smiled Hudson.
"That, my dear James," grinned Elvira, "completely depends on the selling skills and charm of the seller."
"If that's true, Elvira, then you must have made a fortune at the flea market when you were a student."
Elvira shook her head meaningfully.
"It's possible, James, it's possible."
Elvira pressed herself a little closer to the inspector. Hudson did not mind. After all, it made their cover more realistic.
And it was time to concentrate again on what they were doing.

Übung 10: Welche Wörter gehören in die Lücken?
(acrobat, actor, animal trainer, clown, fire-eater, juggler, mime artist, street entertainer)

1. A ____________ has a big red nose and makes people laugh.
2. An ____________ performs in the theatre or in films.
3. A ____________ throws lots of balls in the air and catches them.
4. A ____________ 'spits' and 'swallows' fire.
5. A ____________ never speaks while he is performing.
6. A ____________ sings songs and tells jokes out on the streets.
7. An ____________ jumps and turns in the air.
8. An ____________ performs with horses, elephants or lions, for example.

For the last few weeks an unusual gang of thieves had been at work in the flea markets and shopping areas of London. The crooks dressed up as mime artists and street entertainers, moved close to the tourists during their performances – and then robbed them.
If one thought about it, it was almost a perfect crime. No-one would think it strange if they saw a mime artist in a mask walking down the streets and around squares in broad daylight. Hudson was surprised that no-one had thought of this idea before.
Anyway, the city council was, of course, not at all happy about it. They had received more and more complaints from tourists who had been robbed. The tourist board was afraid – and not without reason – that visitors might stay away because of it.
And since business people, taxi drivers, and snack bar, hotel and restaurant owners made most of their profit from the streams of tourists, they had asked Scotland Yard's best man for unusual cases, Inspector James Hudson, for help.

! ÜBUNG 11

Übung 11: Wie lauten die Sätze? Bringen Sie die Wörter in die richtige Reihenfolge!

1. my The stole money thief all

   The thief stole all my money.

2. will that I'm away tourists afraid the stay

   ____

3. good It very was idea a

   ____

4. the watch artist and Let's mime stop

---

5. to of restaurant A go that tourists lot

In order to look more like a tourist, James Hudson had asked his good friend Elvira Elliot to come with him on his trips around London's famous flea markets. The markets attracted thousands of tourists every day – it was clear that these criminal street entertainers would also feel attracted to them.

However, up to now the inspector's efforts had been unsuccessful. For the last three weekends he had wandered through the flea markets with Elvira, but all of the mime artists that they had seen so far had been harmless.

The tourist board was becoming nervous, and Sir Reginald, Hudson's boss at Scotland Yard, wanted to see results.

Übung 12: Unterstreichen Sie von den beiden Alternativen das passende Wort!

ÜBUNG 12 !

Hudson (1.) shouted/sighed and looked around. It was nearly (2.) midday/midnight and the (3.) narrow/dirty gaps between the individual stalls were getting fuller and fuller. (4.) A couple/Crowds of people pushed past in every direction, (5.) stopped/held in front of individual stalls, haggled about the (6.) prices/prizes and then continued on their way. It was (7.) different/difficult to keep track of everything that was going on in all the hubbub.

A pickpocket would have an (8.) easy/happy job in this crowd. Instinctively Hudson (9.) checked/controlled whether his own (10.) wallet/handbag was still in his pocket.

Yes, it was still there, thank God.
It would not make a very good impression if a Scotland Yard inspector reported that he had been attacked and his wallet had been stolen.
Hudson breathed a sigh of relief and pointed to a corner of the market where the stalls were not so near to each other.
"Come on, Elvira," he said, "let's go over there. This crowd is giving me claustrophobia."
Elvira nodded and followed the inspector.
In a couple of minutes they reached the end of the market. There were a few people selling sofas and cupboards here.
But the inspector was especially interested in a small group of people who were standing near the entrance to a side street.
The people had their backs to Hudson and Elvira, so the inspector could not see what was happening in front of them.
"Let's see what's going on over there," said James Hudson and went towards the group of people.
Loud laughter came from the crowd.
As politely as possible, they pushed past the people who were watching a little show.
A tall mime artist was standing on a small platform and doing a very good impression of Charlie Chaplin, the famous comedian. Although the artist wasn't wearing a bowler hat or carrying a walking stick, you could see who he was imitating immediately.
Elvira burst out laughing when the mime artist pretended to slip on a banana skin. Even Hudson had to smile.

Übung 13: Beantworten Sie die folgenden Fragen zum Text!

1. Were there many people at the market?

____

2. Did anyone steal Inspector Hudson's wallet?

____

3. What were the people near the side street looking at?

____

4. Was the mime artist a good performer?

____

5. Why did Elvira and the inspector laugh?

____

The man with the white make-up on his face really seemed to be good at his job. He didn't look like an ordinary thief who had simply dressed up as a street mime artist in order to practice his dubious profession without being noticed.
"Come on, Elvira," said Hudson quietly to the insurance agent, "the man seems to be harmless. And we're not here to have fun."
"Oh, just a minute, James," begged Elvira. "The boy is really very good."
James Hudson sighed. He simply couldn't refuse Elvira anything. And the inspector had to admit that the mime artist in front of him really knew what he was doing.
Oh well, he thought, a few minutes here or there won't make any difference. After all, today was Saturday and officially he had the day off.

Suddenly, a shout echoed through the crowd of onlookers.
"My wallet! It's gone!"
Inspector Hudson quickly turned around. Just a short distance away from him stood a fat man in a bright checked shirt. An expensive camera hung around his neck and rested on his stomach. Obviously an American tourist.
In despair, the man searched all of his trouser and jacket pockets for his wallet.
In vain.
Hudson glanced at the mime artist, who was continuing his show as if there was nothing unusual going on. He was acting as if all of this was nothing to do with him, but it couldn't be a coincidence. The mime artist probably had an accomplice who stole the onlookers' wallets while their attention was on his show.

ÜBUNG 14 !

Übung 14: Fügen Sie die richtigen Präpositionen ein!
(at, at, for, off, out, to, towards, towards)

Hudson reached 1. __________ his own wallet, took 2. __________ his police badge and walked 3. __________ the mime artist. "Inspector James Hudson, Scotland Yard," he said 4. __________ him in an authoritative voice. "I'd like to ask you a few questions." The mime artist made a theatrical gesture of surprise. A few of the onlookers laughed 5. __________ him, but Hudson was no longer in the mood for jokes.

He took another step 6. __________ the mime artist. But, quick as a flash, the artist jumped 7. __________ the small box that was his platform and kicked it 8. __________ the inspector.

Inspector Hudson nearly stumbled and only just managed to keep his balance. The mime artist used this opportunity to race away down the side street.
A few of the onlookers were still laughing. They probably thought that this was all part of the show.
Hudson kicked the little box aside angrily and started to run after the mime artist.
“We’ll catch him!” Elvira Elliot shouted to the inspector.
Hudson would have preferred Elvira not to take part in the chase – she wasn’t a police officer, after all – but now was not the time to argue with the young insurance agent.
The crooked mime artist was obviously very fit and ran at great speed. Hudson noticed how much he himself was sweating.
But all Scotland Yard officers have to work out regularly as part of their standard training programme. He soon reduced the distance between himself and the mime artist. The inspector heard Elvira running close behind him. The villain wasn’t going to get away.

Übung 15: Welches Wort passt nicht? Finden Sie das „schwarze Schaf“!

! ÜBUNG 15

1. shout, yell, talk, scream __________
2. park, street, alley, motorway __________
3. drink, eat, have dinner, cry __________

4. police, doctor, stylist, ambulance ____________

5. water, fire, flame, burn ____________

6. jogging, weight lifting, sweating ____________

7. fast, slow, quick, speedy ____________

8. punch, hit, kick, throw ____________

9. watch, chase, follow, run after ____________

10. car, bicycle, bus, ship ____________

Suddenly a shadow appeared from a small side alley and blocked the inspector's way. A bald, muscular man with a bare chest and a torch in his hand jumped onto the street.

A fire-eater! thought Hudson, just as the stranger spat a huge flame at him and Elvira.

The mime artist obviously had other accomplices to help him escape. The gang really seemed to be very professional.

But he could worry about that later.

"Get down, Elvira!" shouted Hudson.

At the same moment, the inspector and the insurance agent threw themselves to the ground.

James Hudson felt the flame from the fire-eater's mouth pass directly over his head and burn his hair a little bit.

The same thing happened to Elvira.

"My hair!" she yelled. "He must be crazy!"

At that moment, Hudson jumped to his feet again.

Before the fire-eater could spit out another flame, Hudson hit him on the chin with a well-timed punch.

The man groaned and fell, unconscious, to the ground. Hudson grabbed the fallen torch and put out the fire in a puddle.

They could pick up the man later – now they had to keep after the escaping mime artist.
“Not bad,” said Elvira in amazement, as Hudson helped her to her feet again. “With a punch like that, you could have been a boxer in a circus, James!”
“Your career advice will have to wait, Elvira,” panted Hudson, still slightly out of breath, “first we’ve got to catch the mime artist! I hope he doesn’t have any more accomplices along the way. We’ll end up fighting a whole circus!”
Elvira gave a short laugh, then followed the inspector, who had already started to run again.

Übung 16: Welche der folgenden Aussagen sind wahr?
Markieren Sie: richtig ✓ falsch –

ÜBUNG 16 !

1. The fire-eater was a friend of the mime artist’s.
2. Hudson and Elvira felt the fire on their heads.
3. The fire-eater ran away after Hudson punched him.
4. The mime artist was still running away.
5. Hudson once worked in a circus.

The mime artist had disappeared around a street corner. Hudson and Elvira hurried after him. The inspector and the insurance agent turned the corner – and found themselves in a blind alley.
Fortunately for them, the mime artist had fallen into the same trap. At the end of the street, the criminal was desperately trying to pull a few dustbins to the wall so that he could climb over it.
“Stop right there, my fine friend!” shouted Hudson.
The startled mime artist looked around and swore when he saw Hudson and Elvira.

The inspector fished a pair of handcuffs out of his jacket pocket and went towards the mime artist. Elvira followed him.

ÜBUNG 17 !

Übung 17: Übersetzen Sie!

1. Hudson und Elvira waren sehr überrascht.

____

2. Der Mann fuhr auf einem kleinen Fahrrad.

____

3. Der Künstler konnte nicht entkommen.

____

4. Seine Freunde versuchten, ihm zu helfen.

____

5. Sie rannten sehr schnell.

____

"Not so fast, cop!"
Hudson and Elvira turned round. A tall man in a circus costume was riding into the alley on a unicycle. He was juggling three big clubs.
This just gets better, thought Hudson. First a mime artist, then a fire-eater and now a juggler as well. What would be next? A circus elephant?

"You're under arrest, too," shouted Hudson. "At the very least for insulting a police officer and riding a bike that is not safe for use in traffic."
He had had just about enough of the whole business.

Übung 18: Suchen Sie das Gegenteil der Wörter in Klammern!

However, the (1. fat) ________________ acrobat didn't seem particularly impressed. He (2. slowly) ____________ threw one of his juggling clubs (3. low) ________________ into the air, caught it again – and threw the (4. light) ____________ object at the inspector with all of his strength.

"Hey!" was all Hudson could shout. He only just managed to duck away from the club. With a (5. quiet) ______________ bang it crashed into the wall behind him.

Before Hudson could do anything, Elvira started to run.

"Elvira! No!" shouted Hudson, but it was too (6. early) ________ ______. The insurance agent had almost reached the (7. attractive) ______________ man on the unicycle. Alarmed, the juggler threw the second club at Elvira – but the (8. old) __________ woman stopped it from hitting her with a clever karate kick.

Then Elvira reached the juggler. The horrified man tried to get away on his unicycle, but Elvira was faster.
Full of admiration, Hudson watched as the insurance agent kicked the little cycle out from under the man.
With a yell of anger the man landed unsteadily on his feet. The villain wanted to punch Elvira, but he was too slow this time, too.
Elvira ducked under his fist and sent the criminal flying to the ground with a hard punch.
Half-unconscious and groaning, the man fell to the ground.
"He's had enough," said Elvira with a grin and then looked with concern at her fingernails. "But I nearly broke a nail because of him."
Hudson gave the insurance agent a big smile.
"Great work, Elvira. Did you learn that at the insurance agent college?"
"You learn that, my dear James," grinned Elvira, "when you grow up with three older brothers."

ÜBUNG 19 !

Übung 19: Übersetzen Sie die Körperteile und enträtseln Sie das Lösungswort!

1. Fuß ☐ _ _ _
2. Kinn _ _ ☐ _
3. Knie _ ☐ _ _
4. Zahnfleisch ☐ _ _
5. Ohr ☐ _ _
6. Augenbraue _ _ _ _ ☐ _ _
7. Knöchel _ ☐ _ _ _

8. Bauch _ _ _ _ ☐ _ _

9. Lippe _ ☐ _

10. Schulter _ _ _ _ ☐ _ _ _

Lösung: _ _ _ _ _ _ _ _ _ _

Hudson grinned. Elvira took a step forward.
"Look out, Elvira!" shouted Hudson, but it was too late.
With her left foot, Elvira Elliot stepped on the criminal's third juggling club. She twisted her ankle and fell to the ground with a scream.
A moment later, Hudson was at her side.
Elvira was holding her ankle, which was already quite swollen, and her face was twisted with pain.
"Are you all right, Elvira?" asked Hudson in concern.
"Damn!" gasped the young woman. "I think I've torn a ligament. Why did that idiot have to leave his clubs lying all over the place?"
As carefully as he could, Hudson slipped off his jacket and wrapped it around the young woman's ankle to give it some support. Then he took his mobile phone out of his pocket and dialed 999, the number for ambulance, fire brigade and police in England.

Übung 20: Wie heißen die zusammengesetzten Substantive? Setzen Sie die richtige Ziffer ein!

ÜBUNG 20 !

1. finger	☐	call
2. bus	☐	post
3. alarm	☐	park
4. phone	☐	print
5. washing	☐	clock

6.	car	☐	lights
7.	sun	☐	machine
8.	mobile	☐	stop
9.	sign	☐	glasses
10.	traffic	☐	phone

In a couple of seconds, he got through to a young lady on the switchboard who immediately connected him to the emergency services.

Hudson gave his name, his location and the type of injury. The man on the other end of the line promised to send an ambulance as quickly as possible.

"Sorry to cause you so much trouble, James," whispered Elvira guiltily.

But Hudson just shook his head.

"Don't talk nonsense, Elvira. Without you, these villains would have got away. And to be quite honest, I'm not sure whether I would have been able to stop this fellow and his clubs without your help."

Hudson smiled at the insurance agent again, then he went back to the wall.

The crooked mime artist was still standing there, looking down. He had obviously given up. Maybe he could tell by the inspector's eyes that Hudson was not in the mood for any more tricks. Not now that Elvira had been hurt.

The ambulance siren could be heard in the distance.

Hudson dragged the mime artist over to the juggler, who was still unconscious, and handcuffed them together.

"So, that's that!"

Then he grabbed the mime artist by the collar.

"And you have the right to remain silent, chum …"

Übung 21: Wählen Sie die richtige Alternative!

1. Elvira _______ her ankle.
   a) ☐ injured
   b) ☐ pained
   c) ☐ fell

2. Hudson _______ the Yard what had happened.
   a) ☐ said
   b) ☐ asked
   c) ☐ told

3. Elvira _______.
   a) ☐ was sorry that she had helped Hudson
   b) ☐ did not want to go in the ambulance
   c) ☐ could not stand up

4. The mime artist _______.
   a) ☐ climbed over the wall
   b) ☐ waited by the wall
   c) ☐ helped the juggler

5. In the end, Hudson _______.
   a) ☐ arrested the two criminals
   b) ☐ told the mime artist to be quiet
   c) ☐ put the criminals in the ambulance

Inspector Hudson pulled a face.
Why did all hospitals have to smell so strongly of disinfectant?
Miss Paddington, Hudson's faithful housekeeper, seemed to be thinking the same.

"Just the smell of a hospital makes me feel ill. I hope Miss Elliot won't have to stay in here too long. She's so full of life!" said Miss Paddington, in admiration. "It must be a real nightmare for her to be stuck in here."

"Stop it, Miss Paddington. You're making me feel even worse than I already do," replied Hudson, "after all, I'm the one who got Elvira into this mess."

Elvira Elliot really had torn a ligament during the arrest of the mime artist and his gang and now had to spend a couple of weeks in bed.

ÜBUNG 22 !

Übung 22: Enträtseln Sie die folgenden Definitionen!

1. A place for sick people. *hospital* (ltasphio)
2. A place for tourists to stay the night. __________ (othle)
3. A place to catch a train. __________ (ittsano)
4. A place to buy stamps. __________ (stop cofife)
5. A place to buy food. __________ (pamsuretrek)
6. A place to see a play. __________ (heeratt)
7. A place to have a meal. __________ (treastraun)
8. A place to see a film. __________ (mencia)
9. A place to see interesting old objects. __________ (smuemu)
10. The place where the mayor works. __________ (nowt lalh)

Hudson and Miss Paddington headed for the reception desk.
"Good evening. We would like to visit Miss Elvira Elliot," said the inspector, politely.
The skinny woman behind the window looked up from her computer grumpily and pointed to a small sign.
"Visiting hours were over a long time ago. Can't you read?" she snapped.
"Mmm," was all that Inspector Hudson said, as he calmly took his police badge out of his pocket. He held it up to the window.
"I hope you can read this," he replied dryly, "Inspector James Hudson, Scotland Yard."
It wasn't exactly legal to use his police badge for private purposes – but on the other hand, Elvira had been injured while helping Scotland Yard.

Übung 23: Unterstreichen Sie die fünf inhaltlich nicht dazugehörigen Sätze!

ÜBUNG 23 !

The woman behind the glass raised her eyebrows in surprise. She went to the bathroom. "Oh, inspector," she stammered, "I'm sorry. I had no way of knowing."
The woman took a shower. Then she tapped feverishly on the keyboard of her computer.
"Ah, here we are – Miss E. Elliot, Room Four, third floor, accident surgery department."
Hudson closed his police badge again with a snap. All he wanted was to go home and go to bed.
"Thank you very much. Have a nice evening."
The woman behind the glass nodded. Suddenly she turned around starting to sing a christmas song.

"You're welcome. I live just around the corner. Tell me, has this Miss Elliot done anything bad? I thought she seemed very suspicious. Are you going to arrest her?"

The woman's eyes shone. She was probably hoping to have something to gossip about during her coffee break.
"I'm sorry," Hudson said, "it's top secret."
"I understand, inspector," called the woman through the window, "I won't tell anyone!"
But Hudson and Miss Paddington were already on the way to the lift.
"What an unpleasant person!" hissed Miss Paddington, as the lift doors slowly opened.
Hudson nodded in agreement.
"A real dragon!"
A few moments later the lift doors closed behind them. Inspector Hudson was just able to see the woman at the reception desk gossiping excitedly into the telephone. She was probably spreading the story that there was a dangerous criminal in the accident surgery department.

ÜBUNG 24 !

Übung 24: Welche Gegenteile gehören zusammen?

1.	open	☐ low
2.	interesting	☐ full
3.	dangerous	☐ closed
4.	pleasant	☐ ill
5.	empty	☐ harmless
6.	high	☐ rude
7.	lazy	☐ boring

8. polite ☐ horrible
9. healthy ☐ unpleasant
10. nice ☐ hard-working

The lift doors opened again and Hudson let Miss Paddington go ahead of him.
"After you, my dear."
They stepped into the corridor and knocked on the door of Room Four. Hudson and Miss Paddington looked at each other in surprise when they heard a crash behind the door. A few seconds passed, and then a voice called:
"Come in!"
Hudson opened the door carefully. Elvira Elliot was lying on her hospital bed with a bandage on her ankle and a big smile on her face.
"Oh, it's you, James! And Miss Paddington. What a nice surprise! Come over here!"
"Thank you, Elvira. How are you?"

Übung 25: Wie lauten die Sätze?

1. come her asked in Elvira to friends

____

2. what be They noise could wondered the

____

3. and to bed leg She stay broke in her had

____

4. water you in these Could some put flowers ?

____

5. to is have hospital you boring do It nothing if in

____

Elvira seemed unconcerned.
"Oh, the operation went well – it was nothing. But all this lying around is really getting on my nerves. And I've only been here for one day."
"Oh, you poor thing," sympathised Miss Paddington. "But tell me, you haven't already tried to get up and walk around in here, have you?"
Inspector Hudson's housekeeper looked sternly at Elvira.
"We heard some sort of bump, you know, before you asked us to come in."

ÜBUNG 26 !

Übung 26: Fügen Sie die Übersetzung der angegebenen Wörter ein!

Then Inspector Hudson and Miss Paddington both jumped, because the door to the (1. Schrank) ________________ by the wall (2. plötzlich) ______________ opened.

Hudson couldn't believe his eyes.

Sir Reginald, his (3. Chef) ____________ at Scotland Yard, was standing in front of him.

"Sir Reginald?" gasped Hudson. "What are you doing here? And

(4. warum) ____________________ were you in the cupboard?"

Sir Reginald rearranged his (5. Krawatte) ________ and frowned, looking even more like a bulldog than he usually did.

"Now don't look so horrified, Hudson. Sometimes men do hide in cupboards belonging to (6. hübsch) ________ young ladies, you know."

Hudson and Miss Paddington looked at each other in (7. Erstaunen) __________________.

Elvira giggled like a (8. Schulmädchen) _______________.

"No, seriously, Hudson," smiled Sir Reginald, "when I heard the (9. Klopfen) ___________ I thought it was one of those horrible (10. Krankenschwestern) __________________.

Visiting hours were over a long time ago, you see. Every day I have to deal with some of the meanest criminals in the United Kingdom, but nothing is more frightening than an angry nurse. That's why I quickly hid in the cupboard.
But now let me say hello to Miss Paddington."
Sir Reginald took Miss Paddington's hand, smiled embarrased, and kissed it.
"You look as charming as usual, my dear," he said.
Miss Paddington went red.
"Thank you, Sir Reginald. You're a real gentleman."
Hudson and Elvira grinned at each other while the inspector put the flowers that he had brought with him into an ugly hospital vase.

Übung 27: Welche Verben und Substantive gehören zusammen?

1.	say	☐ a present
2.	watch	☐ one's teeth
3.	pay	☐ a bike
4.	make	☐ hello
5.	give	☐ television
6.	read	☐ some work
7.	brush	☐ a bill
8.	do	☐ a car
9.	drive	☐ a phone call
10.	ride	☐ a book

Then Hudson asked, "What are you doing here, Sir Reginald?"
"Well, I just wanted to thank Miss Elliot personally for what she did yesterday. And also to congratulate you on the arrest of the crooks, my dear Hudson. I know that those three villains must have had another accomplice who was the pickpocket, but he probably won't have the courage to rob any more tourists without his colleagues to help him. The tourist board is very pleased with your work, James and Elvira."
"It was my pleasure, Sir Reginald," said Elvira.
"And I was only doing my duty, Sir Reginald," said Hudson.
Sir Reginald gave a satisfied grunt. For him, this was the highest form of praise.
"Speaking of duty," said Hudson's boss, quietly, "I've already got a new case for you, James."
Miss Paddington noticed the change in Sir Reginald's tone of voice and turned to Elvira. "I can see that these two gentlemen want to talk about official business. Why don't you both go out into the corridor while I give Elvira the little present we've brought for her?"

Übung 28: Welcher Satz enthält die richtige Übersetzung?

1. Hudsons Chef war im Schrank.
   a) ☐ Hudson's head master was in the cupboard.
   b) ☐ Hudon's boss was in the cupboard.

2. Die Aufgabe war schwer.
   a) ☐ It was a heavy task.
   b) ☐ It was a difficult task.

3. Sir Reginald sagte ihnen, warum er da war.
   a) ☐ Sir Reginald told them why he was there.
   b) ☐ Sir Reginald cried them why he was there.

4. Miss Paddington kochte Kaffee.
   a) ☐ Miss Paddington cooked some coffee.
   b) ☐ Miss Paddington made some coffee.

5. Du musst die Bücher nicht jetzt lesen.
   a) ☐ You don't have to read the books now.
   b) ☐ You mustn't read the books now.

Miss Paddington reached into her handbag and produced a stack of detective stories.
"Oh," said Elvira, "are they for me? Fantastic!"
The young woman enthusiastically reached for the books that Miss Paddington had taken out of her bag. Elvira obviously loved detective stories just as much as Miss Paddington herself.
"Ah, 'The Murderer in the Mask'," said Elvira, examining the sensational book cover, "I've always wanted to read that."
"Oh, it's a very good one!" agreed Sir Reginald.

Hudson was amazed.

"*You* read detective stories, Sir Reginald?"

Sir Reginald went red and shook his head.

"… uhm, I …, uuhm, have *heard* that it is very good. My, er, wife told me." Then Sir Reginald took the inspector by the arm and led him through the door into the corridor. Hudson was sure that he had seen Sir Reginald and Miss Paddington wink at each other. The inspector had guessed a long time ago that his housekeeper and his boss had been secretly swapping detective stories for years. However, he had never been able to prove it.

"Well, Sir Reginald," asked Hudson, after he had quietly closed the door behind him, "what is my next case going to be?"

Sir Reginald waved his hand in the air.

"Oh, nothing special, Hudson. I just want you to go on a vampire hunt."

ÜBUNG 29 !

Übung 29: Beantworten Sie die Fragen zum Text!

1. Does Elvira like staying in bed all day?

____

2. Why was Sir Reginald in the cupboard?

____

3. What did the inspector bring for Elvira?

____

4. What was Miss Paddington's present?

____

5. Does Sir Reginald read detective stories?

____

"I beg your pardon?"
Inspector Hudson could not believe his ears. "Are you joking, Sir Reginald?"
But Hudson's boss simply shook his head.
"I'm afraid not. Look at this."
Sir Reginald reached into his briefcase, which he had brought with him into the corridor. He took out a copy of the London Times and began to leaf through the newspaper, not an easy job as the Times was a large, heavy publication.
"Where is it?" he murmured. "Politics, current affairs, arts, sports … ah, here we are! Under 'miscellaneous'!"

Übung 30: In welchem Teil der Zeitung findet man Informationen zu folgenden Themen? ***(arts, business, current affairs, education, miscellaneous, politics, sports, travel)***

ÜBUNG 30 !

1. Information about the government ______________

2. Football results ______________

3. Information about companies and world markets ______________

4. Tips for holidays ______________

5. Things happening around the world at the moment ______________

6. Information about plays, books and museums ____________

7. Information about schools and universities ____________

Sir Reginald held the newspaper in one hand and fished a small pair of reading glasses out of his jacket pocket with the other. Then he put the glasses on and was finally ready to begin.
Inspector Hudson listened with interest as Sir Reginald read the report in a low voice:

ÜBUNG 31

Übung 31: Unterstreichen Sie die neun Substantive, die sich auf Personen beziehen!

"London. In several parks and public areas eyewitnesses have reported the sighting of an unidentified figure dressed as a vampire. The latest victims of this person, who appears to be a madman, were a young couple who came across the stranger last night in the city park. After the villain announced that he was thirsty for the young couple's blood, they ran away. Nobody was hurt during this or other similar incidents in the last few days. The police are certain that they are dealing with someone who is mentally ill. Nothing is known about the identity or the motive of the 'vampire'."

Sir Reginald cleared his throat.
Hudson shrugged his shoulders.
"I don't know, Sir Reginald. It sounds to me as if this really is the work of a madman. And as long as he doesn't harm anyone – after all the whole thing is only printed at the bottom of the page under 'miscellaneous'…"
Sir Reginald grunted and took another newspaper out of his brief-

case. This one was a lot thinner and in a smaller format. Sir Reginald pulled out the newspaper with the tips of his fingers as if he had to touch something dirty.

“If that was all, Hudson, if only that was all. It’s a nice meaty story for some of these other … publications.”

Hudson stared in horror at the newspaper with its huge red headlines.

“The Enquirer? You read this rubbish, Sir Reginald?” he asked in surprise.

“I have to, Hudson, I have to. For professional reasons. Look at this headline.”

Hudson didn’t need glasses to read the enormous headline.

“VAMPIRE TERROR IN LONDON! POLICE POWERLESS!”

The inspector shook his head.

“What a lot of nonsense! Who takes something like that seriously?”

“Oh, a lot of people, Hudson. You’d be surprised. Here, look at this, there’s even a sketch of the so-called vampire. Drawn with the help of eyewitness reports.”

Hudson looked at the crude black and white drawing which showed a thin man with a long face and a long cape. The artist who had drawn the picture had, of course, taken care to particularly emphasize the pointed vampire teeth.

Übung 32: Finden Sie das „schwarze Schaf“!

1. picture, drawing, film, portrait ______________

2. teeth, lips, tongue, head ______________

3. magazine, headline, article, report ______________

4. journalist, reporter, eyewitness, photographer ______________

5. thin, fat, slim, skinny ______________

6. hospital, nurse, doctor, surgeon ______________

7. ill, sick, unwell, healthy ______________

8. concerned, worried, relaxed, nervous ______________

9. terrible, mad, crazy, insane ______________

10. corridor, lift, hall, lobby ______________

"This is ridiculous, Sir Reginald. A vampire in London – what century are we living in?"

"You don't have to tell me, James. But the Yard has been getting concerned phone calls all day. People are asking when the police are finally going to do something about this 'vampire terror'. And the tourist board is getting nervous again. First the crooked street entertainers, now a madman pretending to be a vampire … If this goes on, soon no tourist will have the courage to visit London any more."

Inspector Hudson nodded to show that he understood. He hadn't looked at it like that.

"And you want me to take on the case, Sir Reginald?"

Before Hudson's boss could reply, they heard a high, irritated voice.

"Please leave immediately, gentlemen! Visiting hours are over!"

Hudson and Sir Reginald turned around with a start. A plump nurse was marching resolutely towards them. And she was definitely not in a good mood.

"For heaven's sake!" gasped Sir Reginald. "Let's get out of here!"

Übung 33: Wählen Sie die richtige Alternative aus!

1. Hudson and Sir Reginald were _____ to see the nurse.
   a) ☐ surprised
   b) ☐ glad
   c) ☐ angry

2. The nurse was in a _____ mood.
   a) ☐ good
   b) ☐ bad
   c) ☐ happy

3. The nurse was _____.
   a) ☐ very thin
   b) ☐ a little bit overweight
   c) ☐ tall

4. Sir Reginald wanted to _____.
   a) ☐ leave immediately
   b) ☐ talk to the nurse
   c) ☐ go back into Elvira's room

5. Visiting hours in the hospital were _____.
   a) ☐ only in the evenings
   b) ☐ early in the morning
   c) ☐ finished for the day

Hudson pulled open the door to Elvira's room.
"Miss Paddington! We need to get out of here as quickly as possible! We're in danger!"
But Miss Paddington had already heard the nurse's voice.

She pressed Elvira's hand again and, quick as a flash, grabbed her handbag.
"Goodbye, my dear! We'll come and visit you again soon," she said to the grinning Elvira as she rushed out of the door.
"Thank you very much for the books. And thank you for coming to visit. Goodbye, James! Goodbye, Sir Reginald!"
The two men waved quickly at the giggling insurance agent and rushed along the corridor.
"Sorry, my dear lady!" Sir Reginald called to the nurse. "We've already gone!"
"I should hope so, too! Kindly come back during the normal visiting hours – like everyone else."

Übung 34: Welche Synonyme gehören zusammen?

1. elevator	☐ astonishment
2. sketch	☐ rubbish
3. smile	☐ purse
4. nonsense	☐ lift
5. way out	☐ talk about
6. hurry	☐ drawing
7. wallet	☐ rush
8. notice	☐ grin
9. discuss	☐ exit
10. surprise	☐ catch sight of

A few seconds later Inspector Hudson, Sir Reginald and Miss Paddington were standing in the lift which took them down to the lobby. Sir Reginald was still holding the front page of the Enquirer in his hand.

Miss Paddington looked at it with interest.
"I didn't know that you read the Enquirer, Sir Reginald," she said.
Sir Reginald went red.
"For professional reasons," he replied, "only for professional reasons."
"Aha," said Miss Paddington, meaningfully.
Inspector Hudson grinned to himself.
Then Miss Paddington caught sight of the sketch of the so-called vampire. The old lady raised her eyebrows in surprise.
"Is this your latest case, James?" she asked.
Inspector Hudson nodded.
"Looks like it. Why do you ask, Miss Paddington?"
The old lady looked at Inspector Hudson and Sir Reginald with a smile.
"Well, because I know that fellow!"

Übung 35: Setzen Sie die Wörter an der richtigen Stelle ein! ***(cup, home, housekeeper, town, policemen, pot of tea, living, steaming)***

"Why don't you finally tell us where you know this so-called vampire from …, Miss Paddington?" asked Sir Reginald impatiently.

He had followed Inspector Hudson and Miss Paddington 1. __________. As soon as they had arrived, the old lady had pushed the two 2. ________________ into the living 3. __________ so that she could first make a nice 4. ________________.

"Calm down," said the 5. ________________, offering the police officer the tray with the 6. ________________ cups of tea on it. Sir Reginald and Hudson each took a 7. _________.

"Thank you very much, Miss Paddington," said Hudson. "But now I'd really like to find out how you, of all people, know the vampire that we've been looking for all over 8. _________."

"Well," replied the housekeeper, "I don't really know him. Not personally, at least. Wait, and I'll explain."
Ignoring the astonished faces of the two policemen, Miss Paddington excused herself for a moment and went upstairs to her room.
Hudson and Sir Reginald looked at each other, baffled.
A minute later, Miss Paddington returned. She was carrying a pile of video cassettes.
"Here's our vampire," she said, proudly.
Then she knelt down in front of the video recorder, which was under the television, and pushed one of the cassettes into the slot.
At once, a picture flickered onto the television screen.

ÜBUNG 36 !

Übung 36: Übersetzen Sie und enträtseln Sie das Lösungswort!

1. Pflanze _ ☐ _ _ _
2. Sessel _ _ _ _ _ _ ☐ _
3. Fernseher _ _ _ _ ☐ _ _ _ _ _
4. Kissen _ _ _ _ ☐ _ _

5. Gardine _ _ _ _ _ _ □

6. Brettspiele _ _ _ _ _ □ _ _ _ _

7. Teppich _ _ □ _ _ _

8. Bücherschrank _ _ □ _ _ _ _ _

9. Fernbedienung _ _ _ □ _ _ _ _ _ _ _ _ _

10. Lampe _ _ □ _

Lösung: _ _ _ _ _ _ _ _ _ _ _ _

Hudson and Sir Reginald watched in astonishment as a dark shadow darted across a cemetery. Fog rose from the ground – and it wasn't difficult to see that it came from a smoke machine. Then a spotlight, which was obviously meant to represent the moon, shone onto the man's face. Long, pointed fangs flashed in the light. The vampire with the long, pale face and the combed-back hair looked all around him.

Sir Reginald picked up the newspaper and compared the face of the actor on the television screen with the sketch of the so-called vampire.

"That's our vampire!" he gasped.

Inspector Hudson also looked at the sketch in surprise.

"It really is. A little bit younger, maybe, and a bit taller, but the similarity is amazing."

Then he turned to Miss Paddington again.

"My dear Miss Paddington, what film is this? And who is that actor?"

Miss Paddington shook her head with a grin.

"Oh really, James, you don't know much about popular culture, do you? That's Basil Thornwood, famous for his role as Dracula in the 1970s. He made more than a dozen vampire films for Anvil Studios back then. I've seen them all! I love these old horror movies."

The inspector nodded.

"That's right, I remember hearing the name somewhere. But why should this Mr Thornwood, suddenly start creeping through parks and frightening young couples, thirty years later?"

Miss Paddington looked at the inspector, puzzled.

"I have no idea. Sir Reginald, what do you think?"

ÜBUNG 37 !

Übung 37: Welche Wörter passen zusammen?

1.	famous	☐ light
2.	horror	☐ chair
3.	friendly	☐ car
4.	dangerous	☐ actor
5.	comfortable	☐ friend
6.	good	☐ smile
7.	bright	☐ news
8.	thick	☐ movie
9.	close	☐ fog
10.	fast	☐ criminal

Inspector Hudson's boss looked up.

"Pardon? Oh, I'm sorry, Miss Paddington, could you take a step to the side? You're blocking the screen. It's just getting exciting."

With a giggle, Miss Paddington stepped aside.

"These old films are good, aren't they?"

"They certainly are," nodded Sir Reginald enthusiastically. "Back

then they knew how to make thrillers with simple methods. Ah – here we go!"
Miss Paddington squeezed herself between the two men on the couch.
On the television the vampire, in the form of a bat, was flying around in the room of a beautiful, sleeping woman.
"Oh, how gruesome!" breathed Miss Paddington. "But don't worry – Doctor Van Helsing, the vampire hunter, will be there in a minute!"
Inspector Hudson sighed and took another sip of tea. It was going to be a long evening.

Übung 38: Unterstreichen Sie die richtige Alternative!

Harry McDermott bit (1.) on/into his sandwich. (2.) Half an hour ago/For half an hour he had parked the security van (3.) in front of/ in opposite of the Harris Commercial Bank and was now waiting (4.) of/for the bags of banknotes to be loaded into the van.
Harry pulled a face. His (5.) wife/woman had put tuna in his sandwich again. It was the same (6.) every evening/all evening – why couldn't she give him cheese or ham for a (7.) chance/change? But the McDermotts had (8.) bought/brought a little flat a few months ago which now had to be (9.) paid/paid for. The interest rates were high and tuna was (10.) expensive/cheap.

So Harry took another bite out of his sandwich and looked at the thickening fog which was spreading itself through the dark streets. That was the problem with night shifts – he always had an uneasy feeling, driving through the streets of London at night with a van full of money, but the night shifts were the best paid.

A knock interrupted his thoughts. He jumped. A pale face appeared at the side window of the security van.

Harry was so startled that he nearly choked on his bread. He rolled down the window.

It was Tim, his co-driver.

"Hey ..., you really gave me a fright, Tim," complained Harry. "Do you always have to creep around like that? What's the matter ...?"

Tim looked very bad-tempered. He pointed towards the back of the van.

"Put your stinking fish sandwich away and come and help me. We have to load a couple of extra bags tonight. The bank's business seems to be booming at the moment."

Harry sighed. Of course.

People like him had trouble making ends meet while the banks were raking it in.

ÜBUNG 39 !

Übung 39: Welche Bedeutung haben folgende Sätze? Kreuzen Sie an!

1. Elvira stands on her own two feet.
   - a) ☐ Elvira is indefinite.
   - b) ☐ Elvira is individual.
   - c) ☐ Elvira is independent.

2. Harry and Tim are excited.
   - a) ☐ They have departed.
   - b) ☐ They are nervous.
   - c) ☐ They are exciting.

3. Tell me to my face.
   a) ☐ Don't tell me the truth.
   b) ☐ Tell me straight.
   c) ☐ Tell me how I look.

4. Hudson can defend himself.
   a) ☐ They protested against Hudson.
   b) ☐ Hudson can protect himself.
   c) ☐ Hudson is very defensive.

5. That will be all.
   a) ☐ That's all I have to say.
   b) ☐ That will be great.
   c) ☐ Right now it's nothing.

It really was a great temptation. Driving hundreds of thousands of pounds around, night after night. How easy it would be to simply take one of the bags of money, jump onto the next plane and jet off to South America.

Harry stuffed his sandwich into the glove compartment of the security van and opened the door.

It was actually against the rules for the driver to leave the van. But he could hardly sit there, eating, while his colleague had to work.

Harry McDermott got out of the van and followed Tim. A dozen or so money bags had already been loaded into the back of the armoured van. Half-a-dozen more bags were lying on the ground behind it. Harry could tell at a glance from the shape that these bags contained coins.

Great. Tim had saved the heaviest work until last.

Harry rolled up his sleeves and heaved the first bag up into the back of the van. It was amazing how heavy a bag of coins was.

When he lifted the second bag he was already sweating. Harry felt the tuna sandwich rumbling in his stomach.

Suddenly, the sound of slow, sinister footsteps echoed through the fog.

Harry and Tim looked around at once. Harry's hand felt instinctively for the gun on his hip.

"Who's there?" called Harry.

No answer.

Übung 40: Vervollständigen Sie die Fragen mit einem passenden Fragewort!

1. __________ is the nearest bank?
2. __________ is your favourite actor?
3. __________ time do you finish work?
4. __________ does the next train leave?
5. __________ do you spell your name?
6. __________ are you crying?
7. __________ would you prefer, tea or coffee?
8. __________ sort of car do you drive?
9. __________ was the man in the vampire costume?
10. __________ can I buy an English newspaper?

The footsteps came nearer, but the thick fog muffled all sounds. It was impossible to say which direction the steps were coming from. The two men looked around nervously.

"This is a security van," shouted Harry in a louder voice. "Please keep away until we have finished here."
The sound came closer.
A shadowy figure appeared out of the fog. It slowly walked towards the two men.
Harry screwed up his eyes. All he could see was that the figure was tall and wearing some sort of long coat.
"Looks like a tramp," whispered Tim. "He shouldn't cause us any problems."
"Hey, you! Get lost!" he shouted. "We're armed!"
But the figure continued to move towards the security van.
"He's probably completely drunk," laughed Tim.
However, Harry had an uneasy feeling. Although the figure was coming towards them with slow, shuffling steps, he wasn't staggering or stumbling. Whoever it was – he knew exactly what he was doing.
Harry slowly took his pistol out of the holster.
"Stay where you are! I have a weapon!"

Übung 41: Unterstreichen Sie die zehn Wörter, die falsch geschrieben sind!

ÜBUNG 41 !

Instead of an anser, loud lorghter suddenly echoed through the fog. The two men couldn't stop theirselfes from jumping.
"Boy, he's got some nerve," breethed Tim. He had now pulled out his gun, too.
The figure came closser and finally walked into the pale lite of a street lamp. Harry and Tim court their breath.
Suddenly a tall and evil looking man stood in front of them, waring a long cape. His face was deadly pale, almost blue. But the wurst

thing about him were his black eyes – at least until a smile spread across the sranger's thin lips.

It was then that they saw the flash of two long, pointed fangs.
Harry froze. He suddenly remembered the headline that he had read in the Enquirer that morning!
It was him! The 'Vampire of London'!
It seemed that Tim read the same newspaper as his colleague.
"Th-the vampire!" he stammered.
The figure took another step forward.
Harry McDermott looked at the weapon in his hand. He had seen enough vampire films to know that an ordinary bullet could not harm a vampire.
Harry and Tim quickly glanced at each other again – then they started to run, without even thinking about the money that now literally lay abandoned on the street.
As the men ran off into the night, the vampire's laughter echoed in their ears.

Inspector James Hudson was woken by the gruesome laughter of the vampire.
Still half asleep, he found it difficult to open his eyes.
Miss Paddington and Sir Reginald had watched one vampire film after another. Hudson had managed to stay awake through 'The Vampire of London'. During 'The Return of the Vampire' his eyes had grown heavy and in the middle of 'The Revenge of the Vampire's Bride' he had fallen fast asleep.
By now it was after midnight. Sir Reginald got up from the sofa.
"Thank you very much for a wonderful evening, Miss Paddington," he said, without a trace of tiredness, "but I must be going. It's late."

"It was my pleasure, Sir Reginald," smiled Miss Paddington. "We really must do it again sometime."
Anything but that, thought Inspector Hudson. Then he, too, slowly got up from the sofa to show his boss to the door.

Übung 42: Vervollständigen Sie die Sätze mit einer Präposition!

1. I get _______ at 7 o'clock on weekdays.
2. Please come _______! It's nice to see you!
3. Switch _______ the TV if you're not watching it.
4. I'll just put _______ my coat and then we can go.
5. Sit _______ over there and wait for me.
6. If you don't know a word, look it _______ in the dictionary.
7. Could you please take _______ your wet shoes in the house?
8. My sister is going to pick me _______ at the airport.
9. This book is really good. I can't put it _______!
10. Please fill _______ this form.

Cold foggy air blew towards the two men when Hudson opened the front door.
"Good night, James," said Sir Reginald.
The inspector noticed with astonishment that Sir Reginald had called him by his first name. That only happened when his boss was very relaxed and in an extremely good mood.
"Good night, Sir Reginald. Get home safely. Shall I get you some garlic from the kitchen? Just in case?"

Sir Reginald laughed.

"Don't bother, James. I'll risk it without garlic. I'll see you at work on Monday."

Inspector Hudson nodded.

"Of course, Sir Reginald. Good night!" he said again.

Yawning, the inspector shut the front door after Sir Reginald had got into his car. Then he and Miss Paddington wished each other a good night, brushed their teeth and crawled into bed, exhausted. A few seconds later, the inspector was already asleep. Even in his sleep he was not surprised that he dreamed of vampires chasing him through the fog.

Übung 43: Ordnen Sie die Buchstaben zu einem sinnvollen Wort!

The ringing of the (1. petenohel) ________ startled Inspector Hudson from a deep (2. plese) ________ – he had been dreaming that he was a (3. primave) ________ and someone was trying to (4. likl) ________ him. Sleepily he rubbed his (5. syee) ________ and glanced at the (6. doria) ________ alarm (7. oclkc) ________ next to his bed.

It was 5.30 am.

This was a good start to the (8. ekew) ________.

And an early one, too.
Downstairs, Hudson heard Miss Paddington march to the telephone and answer it.
"Who the hell is this ringing up at such a God-forsaken hour?" she barked into the receiver.
Hudson grinned despite his tiredness.
Then Miss Paddington's voice became quieter.
"Oh, it's you, Sir Reginald. That's another matter, of course. Is James awake? Well, if he isn't, I'll wake him. Hold on a moment, please!"
Inspector Hudson gave another big yawn and rolled out of bed.
"I'm coming, Miss Paddington! Just a minute!"
Hudson put on his dressing gown and slippers, then opened his bedroom door and went downstairs into the hall.
Miss Paddington was already holding out the receiver to him.
"Sir Reginald?" asked Hudson. "What's happened?"
Hudson's boss didn't seem to mind that it was so early. His voice was full of energy.
"Good morning, Hudson! Please come to the Yard as quickly as possible. Our vampire has struck again!"
"Oh?" asked Hudson. "Has he frightened another couple in the park?"
"If that was all, Hudson, I wouldn't drag you out of bed in the middle of the night. No, this time he's robbed a security van and got away with a few hundred thousand pounds!"
Hudson felt his jaw drop.
"What? A vampire that steals money? That's new! Shouldn't he have robbed a blood bank instead?"
"Well, maybe he needs the money for a new castle or something. Please come in straight away."
There was a click as he put the phone down.

Übung 44: Vervollständigen Sie die Sätze mit dem passenden Adjektiv!
(careful, dishonest, foreign, generous, impatient, lucky, reliable, shy, stupid, thirsty)

1. A person who steals is __________.
2. A person who wins the jackpot in the lottery is __________.
3. A person who hates waiting for things is __________.
4. A person who gives her friends lots of presents is __________.
5. A person who is not clever is __________.
6. A person who comes from a different country is __________.
7. A person who wants something to drink is __________.
8. A person who pays attention when he is driving is __________.
9. A person who is nervous when meeting new people is _____.
10. A person who always does what she says she will do is __________.

Hudson replaced the receiver and looked at Miss Paddington.
"It looks as if our vampire has now started robbing banks," he said. "Could you please make me some tea while I quickly get dressed?"
"But of course, James," answered Miss Paddington. "You don't seriously believe that I would let you leave the house without something warm in your stomach?"
Hudson smiled gratefully at his housekeeper, then he rushed upstairs to his room. While he was putting on his suit he could smell the scent of freshly made tea rising from the kitchen.

Übung 45: Wie lauten die Sätze?

1. than tea a There's cup better nice nothing of

____

2. him his asked help Hudson to housekeeper

____

3. need a money does to Why steal vampire ?

____

4. right into Could the come office away you ?

____

5. and on blue tie He new put a his suit

____

"You're an absolute treasure, Miss Paddington," said Hudson shortly afterwards, as he took a cup of steaming tea from his housekeeper. "And I think you'll be able to help me with this case, too – it looks like we're going to need the help of a vampire expert. Will you come with me to Scotland Yard?"

Miss Paddington beamed.

"It would be my pleasure. Let me just carve a few wooden stakes, then we can start!"

Inspector Hudson looked at Miss Paddington, speechless.

The housekeeper burst out laughing.

"Only joking, James, only joking!"

Übung 46: Welche Wörter passen inhaltlich zusammen?

1.	car and	☐ printer
2.	tea and	☐ chair
3.	shoes and	☐ petrol
4.	knife and	☐ money
5.	table and	☐ plane
6.	computer and	☐ sugar
7.	airport and	☐ fork
8.	cinema and	☐ play
9.	theatre and	☐ socks
10.	bank and	☐ film

A few minutes later Hudson was driving his old Bentley through the streets of London. Fortunately it was still very early, otherwise he and Miss Paddington would certainly have got stuck in the rush hour traffic.

But at this time of day there were no delays.

Inspector Hudson used the journey to ask Miss Paddington what she knew about the horror films made at Anvil Studios.

And Miss Paddington turned out to be a walking film encyclopaedia – at least with regard to vampire films from the 60s and 70s. Apparently these were – after detective stories – her second greatest passion.

"Let's see, James, in the late 60s and early 70s – of the last century, as one has to say nowadays – Anvil Studios made dozens of low-budget horror films. Basil Thornwood played the leading role in most of them. I'm sure you must have seen one or two of them on the television late in the evening. Basil Thornwood played almost all of the horror figures that there are: Frankenstein's monster, the werewolf, the mummy – but he is most famous for his

portrayal of Count Dracula. No-one could play the old count as well as he could."
Inspector Hudson nodded. He was not a big fan of horror films, but he thought he remembered having seen this Mr Thornwood as Dracula a couple of times.
"And what does this Basil Thornwood do nowadays?" asked the inspector, as the Bentley stopped at a red traffic light.

Übung 47: Übersetzen Sie die vorgegebenen Wörter!

Miss Paddington shrugged her shoulders.

"(1. Keiner) ______________ really knows. Anvil Studios went (2. bankrott) ___________ at the end of the 70s and up to then Basil Thornwood had (3. verdiente) ___________ a lot of money in his role. He bought a (4. einsam) ___________ country house where he lives a (5. Leben) _______________ away from the public eye. He hasn't given any interviews for (6. Jahre) ___________ and it is said that he has become somewhat (7. seltsam) ___________ in his old age. There is a (8. Geschichte) ___________ that he now thinks he is a vampire and only leaves his house (9. nachts) ___________, if he leaves it at all."

"Very interesting," murmured James, and accelerated again when the (10. Ampel) _________________ turned green.

Half an hour later Hudson and Miss Paddington arrived at Scotland Yard. Although Miss Paddington had often visited the inspector here, she was excited every time she entered this famous building which she had read about in so many detective stories.
At this early hour on a Monday morning, there were hardly any people in the corridors and offices of the Yard. A cleaning lady was pushing her trolley of cleaning materials along the corridor, and greeted the inspector shyly.
Then James knocked at Sir Reginald's door.
"Come in!" came a shout, and Hudson opened the door.

! ÜBUNG 48

Übung 48: Füllen Sie die Lücken mit dem richtigen Wort!
(do, make, take)

1. Please __________ a seat. Sir Reginald will be here soon.
2. I'll __________ the washing-up in a minute.
3. Miss Paddington said she would __________ a cup of tea.
4. He has a secretary to __________ the photocopying.
5. I'd like to __________ a phone call, if that's all right.
6. __________ your time. We're not in a hurry.
7. "We must __________ a plan!" said Hudson.
8. Do you often __________ mistakes?
9. I have to __________ a lot of work today.
10. Let's __________ a coffee break at 10 o'clock.

"Good morning, Sir Reginald," he said, and held the door open for his housekeeper. "I hope you don't mind that I've brought Miss Paddington with me. I thought we might need a vampire expert."
Sir Reginald smiled with pleasure and gestured to his visitors that they should take a seat.
"Not at all, Hudson. An excellent idea. Good morning, Miss Paddington."
"Good morning, Sir Reginald," replied the old lady. "You look very worried, my good man," she added in concern.
"Well, no wonder," sighed the policeman. "There's a madman out there somewhere who's running around and robbing security vans dressed as a vampire. If the press gets wind of this, all hell will be let loose."
"Are you sure that the would-be vampire is behind this, Sir Reginald?" asked Hudson.
"Pretty sure," answered Sir Reginald, and picked up some sheets of paper.

Übung 49: Fügen Sie das passende Adjektiv ein!
(angry, crazy, frightened, long, sensational, serious, sharp, surprised, tall, young)

"Here I have the statements of that 1. ____________ couple and the two security van drivers. The descriptions of this person are the same: 2. ____________, long pale face, a 3. ____________ dark cape – and most important of all, two 4. ____________ pointed vampire teeth. There may be a lot of 5. ____________ people in London but only a few that can be described like that. I don't dare think about how 6. ________ the tourist board is going to be. Fortunately no-one there starts work before nine o'clock in the morning – so I've still got a little more time before the phones here start ringing off their hooks. Despite that, the situation is 7. _______. Thanks to the 8. _________________ newspaper reports about the so-called vampire, the two drivers of the security van were so 9. ______________ that they just abandoned their load. That's why I wouldn't be 10. _______________ if this damn blood-sucker were to strike again tonight."

Hudson nodded his head thoughtfully. Sir Reginald was right. The people's fear of the vampire was a better weapon than a gun.
Suddenly Hudson and Sir Reginald looked up. The smell of freshly made tea filled the office. Miss Paddington smiled and handed each of the policemen a cup.
"I've made you some more tea. Luckily the kitchen is next door."
"Oh, you really are a treasure, Miss Paddington!" smiled Sir Reginald.
Miss Paddington looked down, her face very red.
"If you keep saying that, I'll end up believing it. Would you like a sandwich to go with it, James and Sir Reginald? I quickly made a few before we left home."
Miss Paddington reached into the handbag that she nearly always had with her.
"I've got cheddar cheese and garlic salami."

Übung 50: Welches Nahrungsmittel ist gemeint?

1. A strong-smelling vegetable – vampires don't like it!

2. A long, yellow tropical fruit.

3. Some people cry when they cut up this vegetable.

4. It's made from milk and we spread it on our bread.

5. Wine is made from this fruit.

6. This fruit is very sour, and is often eaten with fish.

7. This small, red fruit is juicy and sweet. We eat it in summer.

8. This vegetable is used to make chips.

9. Bees make this sweet, liquid substance.

10. This cold dessert exists in many different flavours: vanilla, chocolate, nut and many more!

The housekeeper looked expectantly at the two men, but they both shook their heads.
"It's very kind of you, Miss Paddington, but I'm on a diet. My cholesterol level, you know," said Sir Reginald, watching his impressive belly with a smile.
"And it's still a bit too early for me, Miss Paddington," answered Hudson. "My stomach isn't quite awake yet."
"What a pity," said Miss Paddington, and unwrapped a cheese sandwich for herself. "Oh well, all the more for me," she laughed.
Sir Reginald turned his attention back to the eyewitness report and hit the pages with the back of his hand.
"Hudson, we have to do something before the vampire spreads even more panic – and commits more crimes. It can't go on like this."
"Of course not, Sir Reginald. Miss Paddington told me on the way here who the original Dracula was – an actor called Basil Thornwood ..."
"Yes, Thornwood," said Sir Reginald enthusiastically. "A brilliant actor in that role ..."
"The first step would normally be to pay a visit to the production company of those old horror films. That's where we might have found the first clue. But unfortunately Anvil Studios went bankrupt over twenty years ago."
"Um, I haven't told you the whole story yet, James," said Miss Paddington with her mouth full. "Last year an investment company bought the old rights to the Dracula films and re-opened Anvil Studios. As far as I know, they're in the middle of making a new Dracula film. And the studios aren't very far from London."
Inspector Hudson jumped to his feet.
"What are we waiting for?" he shouted. "Come on, Miss Paddington – we're going on a vampire hunt!"

Übung 51: Beantworten Sie folgende Fragen zum Text!

1. Who is Basil Thornwood?

2. Does he still make films today?

3. Where does Basil Thornwood live?

4. Are there many people at Scotland Yard early in the morning?

5. Are Anvil Studios still closed?

6. Where does Hudson decide to go first?

Miss Paddington had not been exaggerating. Anvil Studios were only half an hour's drive from London. Despite this, Inspector Hudson and Miss Paddington felt as if they were entering another world.

Hudson had shown the porter his police badge, and without further ado they had been allowed to drive onto the enormous studio grounds.

Although it was still relatively early in the morning, there was already plenty of activity here.

Film extras in a wide variety of costumes were running to their set or sitting in a corner, smoking a cigarette. A strange sight, for one doesn't sea medieval knights lazily blowing cigarette smoke into the air or drinking a can of lemonade very often.

ÜBUNG 52 !

Übung 52: Welche Gegenteile gehören zusammen? Setzen Sie die richtige Ziffer ein!

1.	entrance	☐	casual
2.	enormous	☐	floor
3.	allowed	☐	exit
4.	famous	☐	ordinary
5.	early	☐	tiny
6.	ceiling	☐	unknown
7.	lazy	☐	start
8.	formal	☐	forbidden
9.	unusual	☐	late
10.	stop	☐	hard-working

From time to time Hudson had to stop the car to let a couple of stage hands go past, carrying aeroplanes made of papier-mâché or house facades made of plywood.

And then there were the stars, who strolled unhurriedly out of their trailers and calmly walked to their sets.

Although Hudson didn't often have time to go to the cinema, he recognised two or three of the faces. By the time the inspector had parked his car in the visitor's car park, Miss Paddington could hardly control her excitement.

"My goodness," she cried, "I'm actually at a film studio! Who would have thought that I'd ever see the inside of Anvil Studios?"

Hudson was still smiling when a young man in dirty old overalls came towards the car.

Ignoring the inspector's astonished stare, he examined the car from top to bottom.

Übung 53: Unterstreichen Sie die richtige Alternative!

"Fantastic," he said. "A Bentley from the early 70s. A bit rusty, but (1.) except of/apart from that in (2.) excellent/terrible condition. Exactly the right prop for our new retro detective (3.) series/documentation. Is the car for (4.) sold/sale, sir?"
Hudson laughed and (5.) nodded/shook his head. He would never (6.) part with/lose his Bentley, at least not as long as it could still pass its MOT.
"I'm sorry, but I don't want to sell my car."
"(7.) What's the matter/What a pity," murmured the young man, and strolled off again without saying (8.) goodbye/hello.
"(9.) Just a moment/Moment, please!" Hudson called after him. "Can you tell me where the vampire films are being (10.) made/taken?"

Without stopping, the young man shouted over his shoulder:
"Vampire films? Sure, Studio 3, Hall B for 'blood'. You can't miss it."
Then he disappeared around the corner of a building.
Hudson looked around. The studio grounds were huge and full of large halls that all looked exactly the same.
He sighed.
"You can't miss it. Great. Then let's start looking, Miss Paddington."
The search for Studio 3 took longer than the journey from London to Anvil Studios. After a good three quarters of an hour the inspector and Miss Paddington finally found themselves standing in front of the right building – but not without first having asked a half-a-dozen people the way.
A small wooden sign announced the title of the film that was being made inside the studio: 'Dracula 2003 – Raving Blood'.

Übung 54: Welches Wort ist das „schwarze Schaf"?

1. huge, long, enormous, massive ____________
2. finally, at last, eventually, possibly ____________
3. disappear, arrive, vanish, go away ____________
4. pointless, senseless, useless, helpless ____________
5. choke, cough, sneeze, sniff ____________
6. announce, shout, say, tell ____________
7. spectacular, impressive, sensational, ordinary ____________
8. bite, chew, gasp, swallow ____________
9. grin, stammer, murmur, whisper ____________
10. near, behind, close, next to ____________

Hudson cleared his throat and knocked on the massive door of the studio, which looked more like a warehouse close up. Rather unspectacular, in fact. Miss Paddington seemed disappointed, too. She had probably expected more shine and glamour.

Hudson knocked again. Nothing happened.

Then Hudson realised that it was actually pretty pointless to knock on the door of a film studio. The film crew would be hard at work inside, and it was unlikely that anyone would hear him.

Without a moment's hesitation, Hudson opened the door and went in with Miss Paddington.

Übung 55: Welche Verben und Substantive gehören zusammen?

1.	make	☐ a message
2.	ask	☐ a problem
3.	knock	☐ a film
4.	solve	☐ a test
5.	wear	☐ a question
6.	tell	☐ on/at a door
7.	deliver	☐ clothes
8.	smoke	☐ a crime
9.	pass	☐ a lie
10.	commit	☐ a pipe

"Aaaand … Action!"
The command came right on cue. For a moment Hudson and Miss Paddington instinctively looked round to see if any cameras were pointed at them.
But the command was directed at a small stage at the other end of the huge hall.
Artificial fog rose from the ground and a young actress hurried across a cemetery with gravestones made of papier-mâché. A man sat behind a big film camera, operating a few levers so that the camera followed the woman running away.
Another young man had a microphone on a long pole which looked like a fishing rod. He was holding it over the stage.
A dozen more men and women were standing around the stage; some were holding strange instruments in their hands, others had notepads and paper signs. A row of ten or twelve dazzlingly bright lights illuminated the whole scene.
Inspector Hudson and Miss Paddington were fascinated, and watched the film recording from a distance.

Then the performance was over.

The young woman had simply run from one end of the fake cemetery to the other. The whole scene had not taken longer than ten seconds.

"Aaaand … Cut!" called a young man with shoulder-length hair, who was sitting on a folding chair.

The director, obviously.

Übung 56: Welche Übersetzung stimmt?

1. Ich brauche 20 Minuten bis nach Hause.
   a) ☐ I need 20 minutes to get home.
   b) ☐ It takes me 20 minutes to get home.

2. Dies ist ein Film von Ray Ratcliff.
   a) ☐ This is a film from Ray Ratcliff.
   b) ☐ This is a film by Ray Ratcliff.

3. Sie ist eine starke Raucherin.
   a) ☐ She is a heavy smoker.
   b) ☐ She is a strong smoker.

4. Miss Paddington war enttäuscht.
   a) ☐ Miss Paddington was disappointed.
   b) ☐ Miss Paddington had disappeared.

5. Er ist sehr an Filmen interessiert.
   a) ☐ He is very interesting in films.
   b) ☐ He is very interested in films.

The lights went out. The artificial fog gradually cleared. The actress who had just been running for her life lit a cigarette, looking bored.
“What, was that all?” whispered Miss Paddington, disappointed. “All that fuss for such a short scene?”
“Fascinating, eh?”
Hudson and Miss Paddington turned.
A young woman in a casual sweatshirt was grinning at the two of them. Her short hair was dyed bright red.
“They say that there’s nothing more boring than making a film.” The girl pointed to the stage.
“And we’ve been trying to shoot that scene since nine o’clock this morning. Something has gone wrong every time – I think that was our eleventh or twelfth attempt.”
Miss Paddington gulped.
“Are you trying to tell me that it takes half a morning to film such a short scene? My goodness, it always looks so easy in the finished film,” said the astonished housekeeper.
“Yes, well, that’s the art of it. By the way, I’m Mary, the ‘best boy’ on this production.”
Hudson looked puzzled. “You … are the ‘best boy’?”

Übung 57: Unterstreichen Sie die fünf Sätze, die inhaltlich nicht zum Text passen!

ÜBUNG 57 !

Mary’s grin became even wider.
“Strange, isn’t it? Not many people are swimming in the lake. We film people have our own jargon. The best boy is the gaffer’s first assistant. He works in a hospital. I think it was originally a shipping term. And the person is always called best *boy* – whether

they're a boy or a girl." "Gaffer?" asked Miss Paddington, at a loss. She went to bed early. Mary burst out laughing.
"A 'gaffer' is the chief lighting technician on a film production. I work as a gardener. I'm still fairly new to the business, but one day I want to work as a gaffer, too. The lighting technician is extremely important for the atmosphere of a film, you see. Be careful of the sharks."

Miss Paddington nodded her head, fascinated.
"Now I finally know the meaning of all of those terms that one sees in the credits at the end of a film."
"But it's fun," said Mary. Then she frowned. "But may I ask who you are and why you're here? Strangers are not welcome on set normally. We try to avoid anything that could delay the filming. And it is said that strangers on set are unlucky …" added Mary.
Inspector Hudson took out his police badge.
"I'm Inspector James Hudson of Scotland Yard and this is my, er, assistant, Miss Paddington. And, to be quite honest, I'm not sure whether our presence here will be lucky for the production or not. Who is in charge here?"
"Police?" she gasped. "Is there more trouble with one of the filming permits? Then it's best if you talk to Ray Ratcliff, the director." Mary pointed to the young man with the shoulder-length hair.

ÜBUNG 58 !

*Übung 58: Vervollständigen Sie die Fragen mit den richtigen Formen von **to be** und **to do**!*

1. Where ________________ he sitting?

2. What time ________________ she begin work?

3. _______________ you feeling better today?

4. When _______________ they arrive last night?

5. _______________ I too early?

6. How _______________ you get to the station from here?

7. How many people _______________ there in your office?

8. Where _______________ you last week?

9. _______________ he very angry when you told him?

10. Where _______________ you go on your last holiday?

"He's sitting over there under the boom."
"Boom?" asked Hudson, puzzled.
Mary laughed again.
"That's what they call the mechanical microphone on the long pole. You can't miss Ray. Just speak to the man who's acting as if he were God."
Mary grinned at Hudson and Miss Paddington again as she slipped out of the door.
"But don't tell him I said that! Otherwise I'll have to go back to working as a 'grip' again!"
"Grip?" asked Miss Paddington, but Hudson shook his head. It would probably take the rest of the morning for Mary to explain the private language of the film world to them.
"Not now, Miss Paddington. First let's go and speak to 'God'."
This time it was Miss Paddington who laughed. Together they walked through the hall, past a pile of cardboard coffins, a church tower made of plywood and a couple of coaches built in the style of the 19th century.

Inspector Hudson stepped up to the young man, who was just shouting at one of his assistants.

"Damn it, do I have to do everything myself around here? I can't work like this …!"

"Excuse me, are you Ray Ratcliff, the director?" asked Hudson, politely.

The young man looked up.

"Who wants to know?" he asked.

Hudson took out his police badge again.

"Inspector Hudson of Scotland Yard. Can I speak to you for a moment?"

ÜBUNG 59

Übung 59: Enträtseln Sie die Definitionen!

1. The person in charge of making a film. __________ (tredrico)
2. Someone who helps other persons at work. __________________ (nassastit)
3. Someone who takes care of another person's home. ____________________ (suekhepreoe)
4. Someone who arrests criminals. _________________ (clameipon)
5. Someone who operates a film camera. __________ (rammenaca)
6. The person in charge of the gate or door to a building or company. __________ (rotrep)
7. Someone who cares for plants. _________________ (gdarneer)
8. Someone who leads a company. _________________ (ngmaare)
9. Someone who drinks blood. _________________ (revmapi)

The director stared at the badge as if he was hypnotised.
Then he got up from his director's chair.
"Er, yes, of course," he stammered. "Come with me. We'll go into the kitchen. No one will disturb us there."
Inspector Hudson and Miss Paddington followed the young man.
Ratcliff seemed nervous, as if he had something to hide.
But Hudson was confident that if the director knew anything about the vampire attacks, he would find it out.
The 'kitchen' consisted of three coffins piled on top of each other in a corner of the old hall. There was a kettle for boiling water. Ratcliff took three teabags and dropped them into three plastic cups.
Hudson noticed the corner of Miss Paddington's mouth twitch. What a barbaric way to make tea! But that wasn't why they were here.
"Well, inspector, what can I do for you?" asked Ratcliff.
The young director seemed to be in control of himself again.
"Right. First of all you can tell me what sort of film you're making here, Mr Ratcliff," said Hudson.
Of course the inspector knew exactly what sort of film was being made in this studio. But he hoped to put the director at ease with this harmless question.

Übung 60: Sind die folgenden Aussagen richtig?
Markieren Sie: richtig ✓ falsch –

ÜBUNG 60 !

1. Ray Ratcliff is happy to see the inspector.
2. The director doesn't want other people to overhear him.
3. The director is not very relaxed.
4. There is a big kitchen in the studio.
5. Ratcliff knows how to make a nice cup of tea.
6. The director seems to know something about the vampire attacks.

The director beamed.
"Well, I'm sure you know the old horror films made by Anvil Productions, don't you?"
"I certainly do!"
This time it was Miss Paddington who interrupted enthusiastically.
"Fantastic films, aren't they?" asked Ratcliff. His smile became wider. His face had an almost dreamy expression.
"Unfortunately Anvil Studios went bankrupt at the beginning of the eighties. The rise of the video market at that time did the film industry more harm than good. Anyway, about a year ago an international group of investors bought the rights to all of the old Anvil movies. We are going to make new versions of all the old classics – and make them more up to date, of course."
"A really excellent idea," nodded Miss Paddington.
"Isn't it?" The director seemed to have completely forgotten that the inspector was still there. His eyes were shining.
"'Dracula 2003 – Raving Blood' is my idea. I wrote the screenplay, too."
"An, er, unusual title," replied Miss Paddington. "What's it about?"
"Oh, Dracula wakes up after sleeping for a hundred years. He buys a techno club just outside London with all of his money. With the help of a mad scientist he develops a sort of ecstasy pill containing blood plasma. And he uses it to make the techno kids and ravers into powerless slaves – an army of zombies who attack London in order to get fresh blood for Dracula."
Miss Paddington gulped. She didn't seem particularly taken with this idea.
"Very, er, interesting," she replied. "But I'm not sure that that is still in the style of the old films."
Ratcliff waved this objection aside.

“Oh, you have to move with the times. The audience today wants violence, blood and hot rave music. Just look at how successful the two ‘Blade’ films were!”

Übung 61: Unterstreichen Sie die Synonyme für die Wörter in Klammern!
(1. had no idea 2. important 3. acting the part 4. wonderful 5. believe it or not 6. careful 7. concept 8. trainer)

Inspector Hudson didn’t have a clue who or what this ‘Blade’ was, but it was now time to ask the key question.
“Tell me, Mr Ratcliff, who is playing the role of Dracula in your new film?”
“Oh, a fantastic American actor called Guy Van Fang. Imagine, that’s his real name. For that reason alone he’s perfect for the part.”
Miss Paddington took a cautious sip of tea from the plastic cup. It seemed just as tasteless to her as the idea of an American playing the role of Count Dracula.
“An American? In the role of the count?”
Ratcliff shrugged his shoulders.
“Oh, nobody will notice the difference. And anyway, we’ve employed a special speech coach to teach Guy how to speak with a real British accent.”

“Would it be possible to talk to this Mr, er, Van Fang? I’d like to ask him a few questions – in connection with the vampire sightings in London.”
Ratcliff choked on a mouthful of tea.
“Vampire sightings?” he coughed. “Oh, right, I read about those. But it’s all just a joke, isn’t it?

"I'm afraid not, Mr Ratcliff. So where can I find the man playing Dracula?"

Ratcliff swallowed again. Then he looked at his watch.

"The cigarette break will be over in a minute, then Guy is filming his first scene for today. If it isn't going to take too long, you can ask him before we start." Hudson nodded.

"That sounds like a good idea."

The young director looked at Hudson once again. He was now much more nervous than before. The inspector was sure that he was on the right track.

Whatever this Van Fang was hiding, he would get to the bottom of it. It was impossible not to notice Guy Van Fang.

The actor walked onto the film set, his cape fluttering behind him. The tall man's long face was made up pale. Long pointed teeth flashed when he opened his mouth.

But when Miss Paddington saw the actor walk into the recording studio, she couldn't help laughing. Van Fang was trying to smoke a cigarette but, with the fake teeth in his mouth, he had to twist his face into a strange grimace. In the end, the actor gave up, threw the cigarette on the floor and put it out with the heel of his shoe.

"Uhhm …, Guy, there's someone here who wants to talk to you," said Ratcliff. Guy Van Fang looked up.

! ÜBUNG 62

*Übung 62: Vervollständigen Sie die Sätze wenn nötig mit **a**, **an** oder **the**!*

1. London is ________ interesting city.
2. What did you have for ________ breakfast this morning?
3. I woke up in ________ middle of ________ night.

4. Would you like ________ glass of wine?

5. I'm tired. I'm going to ________ bed.

6. Is there ________ bank near here?

7. Everest is ________ highest mountain in ________ world.

8. ________ sun rises in the east.

9. I'm really tired. I think I need ________ holiday.

10. Shhh! Don't shout! James has got ________ headache.

"What? Now? Right before we begin filming? I need to concentrate on my role. Can't it wait until later?" he asked.

"I'm afraid not," replied Inspector Hudson, taking a step forward. "I'm Inspector Hudson of Scotland Yard and I'd like to ask you a few questions, sir. It will only take a minute or two."

The vampire gulped. He and Ratcliff quickly exchanged a glance, which did not go unnoticed by the inspector.

There was no doubt that the two of them had something to hide. And it was obvious that their secret must be connected with the vampire attacks.

But then something happened that Hudson had not reckoned with. "I told you right from the start that it was a stupid idea!" shouted Van Fang. Then he grabbed the astonished director by the collar and pushed him against Inspector Hudson.

Both men were so surprised by this sudden attack that they lost their balance and fell to the floor. Miss Paddington gasped. The film crew, who had just been going about their business up to then, looked over in astonishment.

Before Inspector Hudson knew what was happening, Van Fang ran off with an angry expression in his eyes.

ÜBUNG 63 !

Übung 63: Bringen Sie die Wörter in die richtige Reihenfolge!

1. believe could Miss her eyes not Paddington

____

2. inspector floor the pushed the to actor The

____

3. vampire knew director about attacks the something The

____

4. a ask like questions you I'd to few

____

5. last you where night tell you Could me were ?

____

The inspector recovered, but the man playing the part of the vampire had already torn open the door and rushed outside.
Unlike a real vampire, he didn't seem to mind the daylight.
Pity, really, thought Hudson, as he, too, started to run. The inspector did not like being pushed around, especially not by a second-class American actor in a vampire costume. Who, as well as everyone else, was a suspect.
Within seconds, the inspector reached the door of the hall.
He looked around. There was the usual hustle and bustle outside in

the grounds, but there was no sign of the vampire.
Hudson swore as Miss Paddington rushed to his side.
"Are you all right, James? Where did he go?"
The inspector shook his head.
"Thank you for asking, Miss Paddington. The only thing he hurt is my pride. The fellow took me by surprise. But he won't get far. I'll find him if I have to look in every recording studio here."

Übung 64: Unterstreichen Sie die richtige Alternative!

1. It was surprising/surprised how quickly the actor escaped.
2. Hudson was surprising/surprised when the man attacked him.
3. It's an interesting/interested idea.
4. "It's so exciting/excited, being on a film set!" she said.
5. I'm quite tiring/tired. Can we have a rest now?
6. Driving at night can be very tiring/tired.
7. He's such a boring/bored person. He never has anything interesting/interested to say.
8. He's very exciting/excited about his holiday.
9. We were shocking/shocked when we heard that he'd died.
10. The visit to the film studio was disappointing/disappointed.

"We'll find him, James. I'll help you hunt the vampire!" panted Miss Paddington, still slightly out of breath.
James shook his head.
"Sorry, Miss Paddington. He could be dangerous. I don't want to put you in danger."
"Just you try stopping me!" shouted Miss Paddington, and ran off towards the nearest recording studio.
Hudson couldn't stop himself from grinning. It was pointless to

argue with Miss Paddington. Hudson rushed after his housekeeper, who had just opened the door to the nearby studio and disappeared inside.

Without hesitating Hudson burst in behind her – and stopped dead. For a moment he felt dizzy. Miss Paddington had stopped right in front of him. She seemed to be feeling the same way.

! ÜBUNG 65

Übung 65: Fügen Sie das passende Wort ein!
(baseball, earth, everyone, hair, helmet, moon, dust, mountains, recording, space)

The inspector and his housekeeper were standing ankle-deep in 1. __________ sand and staring at the 2. __________, which was rising like a dark blue ball over the 3. __________ of the moon. A few steps away from them stood a man in a 4. __________ suit, who was staring at them in astonishment through his 5. __________.

"Cut!" shouted a furious voice. "Cut! What is going on? Has 6. __________ gone crazy today? The 7. __________ is ruined!"

The inspector looked round, confused.

A man in a 8. __________ cap with grey, shoulder-length 9. __________ and a beard rushed up to them, stirring up clouds of 10. __________ in his fury.

"What do you think you're doing? What do you mean by bursting onto my set? Didn't you see the red light?"
Inspector Hudson swallowed. He wasn't a big cinema-goer, but even he recognised the man with the beard.
It was Stephen Spiegelberg, the famous director.
"Uhhm ..., I'm really very sorry. I'm a policeman and I'm following a suspect. Have you by any chance seen a man in a vampire costume, sir?"
Spiegelberg snorted and glared at the inspector.
"You bet I've seen him. He ruined a scene just before the two of you did. Just follow his footprints in the moondust! And now ... get out of here!"

Übung 66: Welche Wörter stehen in Zusammenhang miteinander?

1. angry	☐	earth
2. beard	☐	apologise
3. ruin	☐	furious
4. sorry	☐	studio
5. planet	☐	moustache
6. cloud	☐	post office
7. book	☐	destroy
8. stamp	☐	sky
9. recording	☐	library

Inspector Hudson nodded his thanks. Then, with Miss Paddington, he followed the footsteps, which could be seen clearly in the 'moondust'.
They could both still hear the director shouting behind them.
"Make your next film in England, he said, you can work in a nice,

relaxed atmosphere there, he said. Hah! You've got to be kidding, George! I'm going crazy here ..."
Spiegelberg continued yelling, but Hudson and Miss Paddington had already left the hall through a back door.
They looked around. The vampire was nowhere to be seen, but the next hall was only a few metres away.
Hudson and Miss Paddington looked at each other quickly, then hurried towards it.
Fortunately nothing was being filmed in this next studio, although it contained a remarkably realistic New York set.

! ÜBUNG 67

Übung 67: Unterstreichen Sie acht Gegenstände, die sich an einer Straße befinden!

Part of Broadway, built of papier-mâché and plywood, was standing in front of a painted skyline. The false facades of the buildings were decorated with billboards and neon signs, which were switched off. There was a street lamp on the corner, and some dustbins between two of the buildings. A tall signpost stood next to a blue mail box. At the edge of the street there was a newspaper stand with real newspapers and magazines on display. In the middle of the fake street there was a yellow taxi, just like the ones in New York.

There were several small holes in the rear window of the cab, which looked like bullet holes. Obviously they were filming a thriller here.
But Inspector Hudson didn't have time to worry about fictional crimes. Not while he was following a real suspect.
"Well, I can't see anyone in here," said Miss Paddington.

"He must have got away again," agreed Inspector Hudson. "So let's go on to the next hall."
The two of them hurried off.
"No Answer from Sub 96! Filming begins on 8.10!" was written on the wooden sign on the door of the next production hall.

Übung 68: Füllen Sie die Lücken mit ***on, at*** *oder* ***in****!*

1. My birthday is __________ the 29th of January.
2. He phoned me __________ the middle of the night.
3. Let's meet __________ 8 o'clock.
4. We normally go on holiday __________ summer.
5. What are you doing __________ the weekend?
6. Mark started working here __________ April.
7. The meeting is __________ midday __________ Tuesday.
8. I seldom watch TV __________ the afternoon.
9. They're going to be away __________ the end of next month.
10. Jane always goes skiing __________ Christmas.

Carefully, the inspector opened the big sliding door and peered into the building. He wanted to avoid ruining another scene and getting into trouble with another director. Although catching a potentially dangerous criminal was more important than wasting a few metres of celluloid, the film industry was an important line of business in Britain.
Hudson did not want to annoy the film people unnecessarily and give Scotland Yard bad press.

But luckily this studio was empty, too, apart from a large submarine standing on a platform in the middle of the hall.
In the dim light of the building it almost looked like a prehistoric monster with its black, shimmering surface.
“Mmm,” murmured Hudson, cautiously approaching the submarine, “an ideal hiding place for a vampire on the run. I think I’ll have to go aboard this submarine.”
“Be careful,” whispered Miss Paddington, as Hudson climbed up a ladder onto the boat. On the top of the submarine he discovered a small round door which led to the interior of the ship.
As quietly as possible, the inspector climbed inside, and was amazed at what he saw.
The props department had done a really good job.
Hudson was now standing in a fully equipped submarine. A periscope came down from the roof. The walls were equipped with radar and radio receivers. The interior of the boat was lit by a red emergency light which gave the rooms a dim, spooky air. A fake submarine for a fake vampire – absolutely perfect. Hudson was sure that Van Fang was hiding in here somewhere – but where?

! ÜBUNG 69

Übung 69: Unterstreichen Sie die neun Wörter, die falsch geschrieben sind, und verbessern Sie sie!

The brige was deserted. The wals and corners, as in real live, were so full of technical instruments that there was no roome for anyone to hide there.
Walking very quitely, Hudson crept throow a narrow passageway that led to the crew’s quarters. Not an eazy job, as the steel wall amplified evry sound.
But there was nobodie in the small bunks in the crew’s quarters.

All that remained was the engine room.
Hudson crept on. The engine room at the back of the submarine was the biggest room. A huge diesel engine – made of plywood – took up most of the space.
There weren't many places to hide here, either. Hudson frowned. Was he wrong? Was it possible that the fake vampire wasn't hiding on this boat after all?
Or had he missed something?
Of course! There was another place on the submarine where Hudson hadn't looked yet.
Very quietly the inspector crept to the front of the boat again, past the crew's quarters and the bridge.
Finally he reached the torpedo room at the tip of the model submarine.
A couple of dummy torpedoes hung on the walls. The torpedo tubes consisted of two long pipes, each of which was closed by a small flap.
Quietly Hudson opened the flap on the left hand side.
The torpedo tube was empty.
Hudson walked carefully to the other side of the boat. Then he grasped the handle of the second flap. In one movement he pulled it open.

Übung 70: Ordnen Sie die Wörter auf der rechten Seite den Begriffen auf der linken zu!

1. say	a) ☐	chilly, icy, freezing
2. walk	b) ☐	cheerful, pleased, delighted
3. quiet	c) ☐	murmur, whisper, stammer
4. cold	d) ☐	little, tiny, slight

5. hot	e)	☐	creep, march, stroll
6. pretty	f)	☐	huge, enormous, large
7. angry	g)	☐	silent, noiseless, soft
8. happy	h)	☐	boiling, heated, roasting
9. big	i)	☐	beautiful, attractive, lovely
10. small	j)	☐	furious, cross, annoyed

Guy Van Fang, the man playing the vampire, was lying head first in the narrow shaft, trying as hard as he could to climb through the tube to freedom. "Not so fast …," shouted Hudson.

He grabbed the struggling man by the ankle.

But Van Fang was stronger than Hudson had thought. In desperation, the actor pulled himself further forwards. Hudson's hand slipped and he was left holding the actor's shoe.

Before the inspector could do anything about it, Van Fang slipped out of the opening of the torpedo tube and was free.

Without hesitating, Hudson forced his way into the narrow tube – but it was too late.

Guy Van Fang had already jumped to the ground and was escaping through the hall.

But he hadn't reckoned Miss Paddington.

The determined old lady had seen everything and suddenly jumped out from behind a large box.

"Stop right there, you good-for-nothing vampire!" she shouted, blocking the actor's path.

Van Fang tried to avoid the old lady, but Miss Paddington whirled her handbag in the air and hit the escaping actor on the head as hard as she could.

With a yell of pain the vampire fell to the ground, where he lay groaning and holding his jaw.

"Well done, Miss Paddington," called the inspector.

Then he struggled out of the narrow torpedo tube and jumped to the ground, too.

"Doctor Van Helsing and his wooden stakes are nothing compared to you and your handbag."

Miss Paddington beamed with pride.

Übung 71: Beantworten Sie folgende Fragen zum Text!

ÜBUNG 71 !

1. What was the film in the next studio about?

___

2. Did the submarine look realistic on the inside?

___

3. Did Hudson make a lot of noise inside the submarine?

___

4. Where was Van Fang hiding?

___

5. How did Miss Paddington stop the vampire from escaping?

___

Looking very ashamed, Guy Van Fang stood in front of Inspector Hudson, Miss Paddington and Ray Ratcliff.

The vampire really was a sorry sight. His cape was dirty and torn, his left shoe was missing, and – worst of all – Miss Paddington's handbag attack had cost him his right fang.

Inspector Hudson had marched the fake vampire all away across the studio grounds back to Hall 4.

Then he had sent the rest of the astonished film crew outside. Ray Ratcliff and Guy Van Fang had a lot of explaining to do.

"All right," began the inspector, "what can you tell me about these vampire attacks? I'm particularly interested in the little matter of the security van, gentlemen."

The director and his leading actor gave each other a quick look.

"I told you right from the beginning that it was a stupid idea. It was obvious that we'd never get away with it," spat Van Fang at the director.

"Oh, rubbish," Ratcliff snapped. "It was a great idea. All advertising is good advertising!"

"Yeah, fantastic! And now I'm going to be sent to prison for it!"

ÜBUNG 72 !

Übung 72: Finden Sie für die britischen Begriffe auf der linken Seite das amerikanische Gegenstück!

1.	prison	☐ sidewalk
2.	taxi	☐ freeway
3.	lift	☐ truck
4.	pavement	☐ jail
5.	rubbish	☐ vacation
6.	petrol	☐ cab
7.	lorry	☐ garbage
8.	motorway	☐ elevator
9.	holiday	☐ apartment
10.	flat	☐ gasoline

Hudson was only just able to stop the fake vampire from going for the director's throat, broken fang or no broken fang. The inspector grabbed the actor by his collar and held him back.

"Calm down, gentlemen! Why don't you start from the beginning? Then we'll see who has to go to prison for what."
Van Fang gradually calmed down.
"OK, I admit everything. I was the vampire who frightened that couple in the park. The whole thing was Ray's idea. He thought it would be an excellent idea for me to go around frightening people long before the film was finished. As a secret promotion tour, as it were. People were supposed to talk about nothing but vampires – and then be so fascinated that they'd rush to the cinemas as soon as 'Dracula 2003' was released."
The director nodded.
"It's true. But we didn't have anything to do with the robbery. We didn't want to harm anyone with our promotion. Just create a bit of interest in our film."
"I understand," nodded the inspector. "And do you know what? I even believe you. But if you don't have a watertight alibi I have no choice but to arrest you and take you to a police cell."

Übung 73: Unterstreichen Sie die richtige Alternative!

ÜBUNG 73 !

Ratcliff went pale – even paler than Van Fang under his horror make up.
"But … (1.) what is with/what about our film?" he stammered. "We can't (2.) afraid/afford a long break in filming!"
"You should (3.) have/had thought about that sooner, (4.) should/shouldn't you?" replied the inspector.
"Oh dear," said Miss Paddington, (5.) sorrowfully/cheerfully. "The poor young people. They'll all (6.) loose/lose their jobs, won't they? That nice girl, Mary, too."
Hudson shrugged (7.) his shoulders/himself.

"I'm afraid there's (8.) anything/nothing I can do, Miss Paddington. (9.) When/Unless our would-be vampire here has a watertight alibi for the night of the robbery."
Ratcliff (10.) pricked up/picked up his ears.

"When exactly was the security van robbed?" he asked hopefully.
"On Sunday night," answered the inspector.
The director suddenly beamed.
"Well, that's great! We have our alibi! Inspector, I can prove to you that Guy didn't have anything to do with the robbery. We were filming all that night."
"That's right!" remembered Van Fang. "In the cemetery!"
"In the cemetery?" asked the inspector.
The director coughed nervously.
"Well, it wasn't exactly legal, but that doesn't matter anymore. To make the opening scene of our film look more realistic, I secretly filmed it with a video camera in a real cemetery. Without a filming permit, of course," he added with a wink.
Then he quickly walked to the exit of the hall and signalled to the others that they should follow him.
"Please come with me," he called. "The video equipment and the tape are still in my trailer."
Doubtfully, Inspector Hudson and Miss Paddington followed the young director and the fake vampire across the studio grounds.
"Do you really live in a trailer?" asked Miss Paddington in surprise.
Ray Ratcliff shrugged.
"Sure. Most of us do, including the actors, by the way. Sleeping in a trailer on set saves a lot of travelling time. Film studios are not normally located in the city centre, are they? And anyway, you wouldn't believe how comfortable these trailers are nowadays."
Ratcliff walked up to a shiny, silver, American-style trailer,

unlocked the door and asked them to come in.
Hudson and Miss Paddington could hardly believe their eyes. The trailer really was very roomy. The interior was divided into a small sleeping area and a small, fully furnished living room. There was even a tiny kitchen at the back.
It would be really nice to live here – apart from the terrible mess. Everywhere they looked there were dirty cups and plates, and the little sofa was overflowing with cardboard boxes from a pizza delivery service. There were clothes lying under the sofa and piles of tattered film magazines on the bed.

Übung 74: Übersetzen Sie und enträtseln Sie das Lösungswort!

1. Unordnung _ _ □ _
2. Vergnügen _ □ _
3. Schlafzimmer □ _ _ _ _ _ _
4. bequem _ _ □ _ _ _ _ _ _ _ _
5. Teller _ _ □ _ _
6. Bildschirm _ _ □ _ _ _
7. Küche _ □ _ _ _ _ _
8. faszinieren _ _ _ _ _ □ _ _ _
9. gefrieren _ _ □ _ _ _

Lösung: _ _ _ _ _ _ _ _ _

"It looks as if you urgently need a housekeeper, Mr Ratcliff," said Miss Paddington, shaking her head. "What an awful mess!"

Ratcliff was unconcerned.

"Oh, I only come in here to sleep, anyway. And to eat."

Then he began to search his trailer for the video camera. Because of the mess, it was a good five minutes before the director found the camera under a pile of dirty washing.

He held it up proudly.

"Here it is! My ticket to freedom!"

"*Our* ticket to freedom," added Guy Van Fang.

"Let's wait and see." The inspector raised an eyebrow, sceptically.

But Ratcliff was confident.

"You'll see, inspector," he said, and set about connecting the camera to the television set in the living room area with a cable.

A few seconds later, a picture flickered onto the screen. Hudson and Miss Paddington looked at it, wondering what was to come next.

Übung 75: Setzen Sie den richtigen Begriff in die Lücke!

(bathroom, beach, border, camping site, cemetery, forest, garage, mountain, pub, stadium)

1. A place to have a shower or wash. ____________
2. A place to have a drink in the evening. ____________
3. A place to keep your car. ____________
4. A place where dead people are buried. ____________
5. A place where you can sleep in a tent. ____________
6. A place to watch a football match. ____________

7. A place to sit on the sand, sunbathe and swim. ____________

8. A place with a lot of trees. ____________

9. A place to go skiing. ____________

10. A place that divides two countries. ____________

They saw an old cemetery through clouds of thick fog.
"Ah, there's nothing like filming on location," said Ratcliff. "It's never as realistic as this when you film in a studio."
The camera panned once across the whole cemetery and then zoomed in on a dark figure staggering through the fog. It was Guy Van Fang in his Dracula costume.
"This is going to be my opening scene," said the actor, proudly. "Count Dracula wakes up after a hundred years and climbs out of his grave."
"This doesn't prove anything, I'm afraid," said the inspector. By now he was certain that the two young men were innocent – at least with regard to the security van robbery. But they would have to come up with something better than this if they didn't want to be arrested.
"Wait, inspector," said Ratcliff, and pressed a small button on the video camera.
Instantly a couple of numbers flickered onto the top corner of the TV screen. His modern video camera had obviously also recorded the time and date that the film had been made.
Hudson screwed up his eyes in order to be able to read the tiny numbers better.
But there was no doubt: the video recording had definitely been made on the Sunday evening, at exactly the same time as the robbery of the security van.

Hudson took a deep breath.

"Good, you've convinced me, Ratcliff. This proves without a doubt that you have an alibi for the time of the crime."

Relief spread across the faces of Ray Ratcliff and Guy Van Fang.

"Does that mean we're off the hook?" asked the actor.

Hudson looked sternly at the man.

"Well, there's still the fact that you went around frightening people while dressed as a vampire. And then we have the matter of making a film in a public cemetery without a permit."

Hudson looked at the horrified faces of the two men. He smiled to himself. The two of them had clearly gone too far with their little advertising campaign. But they had not actually wanted to harm anyone by doing so.

"On the other hand," added Hudson after a pause, "those are minor crimes for which Scotland Yard is not really responsible. I'll have to report everything, of course … but it's just possible that I might forget to do so while hunting for the real criminal. I can't think of everything, can I?"

Übung 76: Wählen Sie die richtige Alternative aus!

1. Ratcliff filmed the first scene of his movie ________.
   a) ☐ on Saturday evening
   b) ☐ without a permit
   c) ☐ in a studio just outside London

2. The inspector saw the date that the film was made ________.
   a) ☐ on a piece of paper in the trailer
   b) ☐ written on the video cassette
   c) ☐ on the TV screen

3. Ratcliff and Van Fang ________.
   a) ☐ don't have a good alibi
   b) ☐ had nothing to do with the robbery
   c) ☐ make films on location every weekend

4. Inspector Hudson decided ________.
   a) ☐ not to arrest the two men
   b) ☐ to report the crime to his boss
   c) ☐ to make sure that Ratcliff has a filming permit

5. The 'advertising campaign' ________.
   a) ☐ was Ratcliff's idea
   b) ☐ was very dangerous and harmed a lot of people
   c) ☐ was good for the film industry

Ray Ratcliff was so happy that he almost flinged his arms around the inspector's neck. Guy Van Fang felt relieved and was grinning all over his face.

"Oh, thank you, inspector," said the director. "How can I ever make it up to you?"

Inspector Hudson looked sternly at the young man.

"Well, by not starting any more 'advertising campaigns' like this in the future, Mr Ratcliff."

The director nodded eagerly.

"Of course not, inspector!"

"It was a stupid idea, anyway," added Van Fang.

The director turned to his star.

"Oh yeah, really?" he snapped, angrily. "But at the beginning you loved it!"

"But I had no idea then how much trouble it would cause me! You nearly got me sent to prison with your stupid idea!"

Übung 77: Tragen Sie die Vergangenheitsform der angegebenen Wörter ein!

The director and his leading man seemed to have completely forgotten that Hudson and Miss Paddington (1. be) __________ still there. They (2. begin) __________ shouting and swearing at each other furiously.

Inspector Hudson (3. give) __________ his housekeeper a sign. The two of them (4. leave) __________ the trailer and (5. go) __________ back outside.

Inside the trailer, the argument (6. be) __________ still going on. Miss Paddington (7. smile) __________ at the inspector.

“It was really nice of you not to arrest those two, James. They might be a bit strange, but they’re still good boys. And I would have been sorry if that nice girl, Mary, (8. lose) __________ her job because her boss was in prison.”

“That’s just what I (9. think) __________, Miss Paddington. And I think Mr Ratcliff and Mr Van Fang have learnt their lesson.”

“Then at least one good thing (10. come) __________ of our little trip, James. It’s just a pity that you’ll have to begin your investigations again from the beginning now.”

Inspector Hudson smiled.
"Oh, I wouldn't say that, Miss Paddington. I've already got a new idea …"
Elvira Elliot was over the moon when she received the inspector's phone call. She had been lying restlessly in her hospital bed all day long. All this lying around and doing nothing was just not her cup of tea. The young insurance agent needed action, she needed a task, even if it was only some comparatively simple internet research.

Übung 78: Was bedeuten folgende Redewendungen?

1. Elvira was over the moon.
   a) ☐ She often woke up at night.
   b) ☐ She was very pleased.
   c) ☐ She was very surprised.

2. It was not her cup of tea.
   a) ☐ It was not the sort of thing she enjoyed.
   b) ☐ The cup of tea belonged to someone else.
   c) ☐ She preferred coffee.

3. Hudson will call you back in a minute.
   a) ☐ He'll do it immediately.
   b) ☐ He'll do it in the future.
   c) ☐ He'll do it minutely.

4. The nurse is a real pain in the neck.
   a) ☐ She has injured her neck.
   b) ☐ She is a very irritating person.
   c) ☐ She has got a headache.

Mobile phones were, of course, not allowed in the hospital, but Elvira had switched from the ringing tone to 'vibrate' and hidden the small gadget under her pillow. When Hudson called her on her mobile she was immediately keen to help.
"Give me half an hour, James," Elvira said into the phone. "It won't take me much longer than that."
James Hudson, on the other end of the line, thanked her.
Elvira Elliot activated the infra-red connection of her laptop with her high-tech mobile phone.

Übung 79: Enträtseln Sie die folgenden Definitionen!

1. A small, portable computer. __________ (toppal)
2. A machine to print documents. __________ (trepnir)
3. A phone that you can carry in your pocket. __________ (blimoe)
4. Use this to type words into a computer. __________ (yardboke)
5. Use this to connect your computer to the Internet. __________ (medom)
6. The World Wide Web! __________ (trInteen)
7. Use this 'animal' to click on things on your screen. __________ (sumoe)
8. A fast way to send someone a letter. __________ (le-ami)

It only took a couple of seconds for her to be connected to the Internet. Elvira didn't know how she had managed to do her work before the apparently limitless source of information, the World Wide Web, had existed.
'World Wide Web' – the name not only sounded good, it was also absolutely accurate. Within seconds she had opened her browser and got onto one of the numerous search machines. Then she typed

in just one name: BASIL THORNWOOD.
Elvira pressed the ENTER key – and instantly a long list appeared on the screen of her laptop.
The list displayed every homepage in the Internet on which the name of the former Dracula star appeared. Elvira gave a sigh, but she had learned not to be put off by the large number of results of an Internet search.
It was normally enough to click on just the first three or four entries in order to get a useful result.
Elvira clicked on the first entry. Although the connection via her mobile phone was somewhat slower than the one she was used to at home, it still only took a couple of seconds for something to appear on the screen.
The insurance agent got a slight shock when the screen of the small laptop suddenly turned black.
For a moment Elvira thought that the computer had crashed, but suddenly the photo of a weather-beaten, moss-covered gravestone appeared on the monitor.
Elvira jumped when, very suddenly, the sound of a door creaking, followed by a blood-chilling scream, could be heard through the little loudspeaker on the laptop.
The programmer of this website had obviously taken a lot of trouble to use as many 'multi-media' tricks as possible.

Übung 80: Fügen Sie die Übersetzung der angegebenen Wörter ein!

ÜBUNG 80 !

A moment later, the door to Elvira's room was torn open.

The bossy nurse, who had thrown James Hudson and the others out

the day before, put her (1. Kopf) __________ around the door.

"What was that (2. Schrei) __________?" asked the nurse, sounding concerned. "Is (3. alles) __________ OK?"

Just in time, Elvira managed to (4. verstecken) __________ her mobile phone under the (5. Bettdecke) __________.

"Hhmm, yes, I'm fine," she said, (6. schnell) __________. "I'm, uuhm …, just watching a film on my laptop. A, er, horror film!"

The nurse shook her head disapprovingly.

"All these modern gadgets," she grumbled. "In the old days the (7. Patienten) __________ used to just lie in bed and (8. lesen) __________. If you have to watch rubbish like that, then at least turn the (9. Lautstärke) __________ down. This is a hospital, not a (10. Kino) __________!"

"Of course. I'm sorry," said Elvira, and switched off the sound on her laptop completely. "It won't happen again!"

"Hmmm, I should hope not!" growled the nurse, before closing the door behind her.

Elvira waited until the nurse's heavy footsteps had died away. Then she breathed a sigh of relief.

She didn't want to think about how that dragon would have reacted if she had found the mobile phone …

Elvira looked at the screen again. In the meantime the whole homepage had been downloaded. It had obviously been put on the net by a fan of old British horror films. Half-a-dozen hyperlinks had been written on the gravestone in a bloody handwriting.

Elvira positioned the mouse on 'The Vampire of London' and then clicked with the left mouse button to activate the hyperlink.
A couple of seconds later, a new page filled the screen, containing a summary of the story and a few photos from the old film. She knew that this old movie was one of Basil Thornwood's most famous films.
And there it was: after she had scrolled down to the bottom of the page, she found another hyperlink to a biography of Basil Thornwood.
Elvira reached into the drawer of her bedside table and took out a small pair of reading glasses – which she had never worn in the presence of James Hudson – and began reading the text.
What she found out about Thornwood, the Dracula star, on this page was enough to make her blood freeze …

Übung 81: Finden Sie die Synonyme!

1.	find out	☐ admirer
2.	freeze	☐ best known
3.	biography	☐ shut
4.	most famous	☐ discover
5.	switch off	☐ shriek
6.	close	☐ turn to ice
7.	fan	☐ eager
8.	scream	☐ life story
9.	position	☐ turn off
10.	keen	☐ place

"Really?" said Inspector Hudson, glancing at Miss Paddington. "That is extremely interesting, Elvira. And worrying. Thank you very much. I owe you one. Yes, I'll do that. Goodbye, Elvira." Hudson ended the call and put his mobile phone back into his jacket pocket.

Miss Paddington looked at him with interest. They were both still standing on the grounds of Anvil Studios. The colourful hustle and bustle around them had, however, more or less died down by now. The sun was just setting, and most of the day's filming seemed to have finished.

"Well," asked Miss Paddington. "What have you found out, James? What did you want Elvira to do, anyway?"

The inspector nodded towards his old Bentley, which was now standing all alone on the visitors' car park.

"Come on, Miss Paddington, I'll tell you about it on the way. First of all, Elvira sends her love."

"Oh, thank you," smiled Miss Paddington. "How is she?" "Oh, she seems fine," answered Hudson. "I have a feeling that having to lie in bed is causing her more problems than her injured leg."

Miss Paddington burst out laughing as Hudson held the car door open for her.

"Yes, I can imagine that."

Übung 82: Übersetzen Sie!

1. Er schuldet mir etwas Geld.

____

2. Mein Handy klingelte und ich ging dran.

____

3. Nimm das Geld und steck es in deine Tasche!

---

4. Es lohnt sich nicht, noch länger zu warten.

---

5. Wir müssen uns über Basil Thornwood informieren.

Hudson walked round to the other side of the car and got in. While starting the engine, he continued his story.
"Now that our friend Guy Van Fang is no longer suspected of robbing the security van, I realise that there's another talented Dracula actor ..."
"Do you mean Basil Thornwood?" Miss Paddington asked in astonishment.
Hudson nodded.
"Exactly. Of course I don't know if he has anything to do with the affair. I wasn't sure if the man was even still alive. He's not exactly young any more."

Übung 83: Unterstreichen Sie die Synonyme für die Ausdrücke im Text!
(1. in his most successful period 2. older than 3. for a very long time 4. was no longer seen on TV or in newspapers, etc 5. try to become famous again 6. failed 7. sorrowfully 8. these days)

! ÜBUNG 83

Miss Paddington nodded again.
"That's true. Even in his heyday as Count Dracula he must already

have been over thirty. And that was in the seventies. And I haven't heard or read anything about him for ages."
"No wonder," nodded Hudson as he drove the car across the studio grounds. "Elvira found out on the Internet that Basil Thornwood retired from the public eye years ago. In the late eighties he tried to make a comeback as a vampire in a few cheap video productions, but wasn't successful."
"People today just don't understand classic entertainment," said Miss Paddington, regretfully. "Maybe our Mr Ratcliff is right, and nowadays people only want blood, loud music and special effects on the cinema screen."

"It's possible," replied the inspector, but at that moment he was not very interested in the development of the entertainment market.
"Anyway," he continued, "Basil Thornwood finally retired from the film business, a disappointed man. He bought a little castle in the country with the rest of his money, and since then he has lived there in complete isolation. The inhabitants of the nearby village say that Thornwood has gone mad and now actually believes that he is a vampire."
"Really? That's incredible!" exclaimed Miss Paddington.
"There was a reporter the year before last who thought so, too. According to Elvira's information, and despite all the warnings, he dared to go to Thornwood's castle to try and interview the old actor …"
"And did Thornwood let the man in?" asked Miss Paddington, curiously.
Hudson nodded his head.
"Oh yes, he let him in – wearing a set of artificial vampire teeth! Thornwood actually attacked the reporter and bit the poor fellow. The man just managed to get away in time. The wound on the reporter's neck had to be stitched afterwards. With 17 stitches."

Übung 84: Welche Gegenteile gehören zusammen?

1. attack	☐	answer
2. country	☐	cowardly
3. question	☐	future
4. simple	☐	defend
5. public	☐	reveal
6. alive	☐	city
7. past	☐	natural
8. hide	☐	complicated
9. artificial	☐	dead
10. brave	☐	private

Miss Paddington put her hand to her mouth in horror.
"Oh my goodness, that's terrible. It seems as if Basil Thornwood really has lost his mind."
"Obviously," murmured Hudson, as he drove his Bentley along the country road. "Let's just hope that he's having one of his clear spells at the moment ..."
The housekeeper looked questioningly at the police inspector.
"What for, James?"
"Quite simple," replied Hudson. "We're going to pay old Mr Thornwood a visit ..."

Although Elvira Elliot had given the inspector precise directions, he still had difficulties in finding Basil Thornwood's castle. Darkness had fallen across the country and there was thick fog on the roads.
After they had been driving along the country roads for a while, not really sure where they were, Inspector Hudson finally discovered the lights of a small village ahead of him.

He drove his Bentley along the empty main road of the village. There was no one on the street who he could ask the way.
In the end, Hudson parked in front of a small pub, the only public building that was still open.

Übung 85: Welche Verben und Substantive gehören zusammen?

1. park	☐ someone's birthday
2. find	☐ to the radio
3. spend	☐ a hole
4. pour	☐ a car
5. listen	☐ a letter
6. hear	☐ the way
7. make	☐ a drink
8. dig	☐ an appointment
9. remember	☐ money
10. sign	☐ a noise

Miss Paddington giggled in amusement.
"What's so funny, Miss Paddington?" asked the inspector.
Miss Paddington smiled at the inspector as they went up the steps to the pub.
"Oh, it's just that I feel as if I'm in a real horror film. The little village, the fog, the unsuccessful search for the castle … I bet the customers in the pub will warn us not to enter Basil Thornwood's castle at night."
Inspector Hudson looked at his housekeeper. He hadn't thought of it like that at all.

Übung 86: Ordnen Sie die Buchstaben zu einem sinnvollen Wort!

ÜBUNG 86 !

Then he opened the door. The fog inside the small pub seemed to be even thicker than (1. dositue) _________. Here, however, it was only (2. tragetcie) _________ smoke, which was wafting through the room in thick (3. dolscu) _________.

The air was filled with the murmuring of the (4. moctresus) _________, who became somewhat quieter as the inspector and Miss Paddington (5. deklaw) _________ towards the bar. Curious eyes (6. woloflde) _________ them.

" (7. sucExe) _________ me," said the inspector politely, beckoning to the pub-owner. "I'm (8. ridafa) ________ we're lost. Could you tell us the best way to get to Mr Basil Thornwood's house?"

The pub-owner raised his eyebrows in surprise. All at once, the murmuring in the room seemed to stop.
Miss Paddington grinned.
"You see, James?" she said quietly. "What did I tell you?"
The pub-owner almost dropped the glass that he was drying.
"Y-you want to go to Thornwood's castle? In the middle of the night?"
Hudson nodded politely. "Yes, I do."
The pub-owner looked meaningfully at the inspector.

"I, … uhhm …, of course I can tell you the way, sir, but wouldn't you rather wait until tomorrow? Until the sun rises?"
Miss Paddington gave the inspector a quick dig in the ribs. Hudson did his best to ignore her. But by now he also felt as if he was in an old horror movie.
"I'm afraid, my dear fellow, that what I have to discuss with Thornwood can't wait," said Hudson. "Could you please tell us the way to the castle?"
Unwillingly, the pub-owner nodded and scribbled a little sketch onto the back of a beer mat. If Hudson had read the map correctly, then the castle was not far away. Without the fog he probably would have been able to see it, even in the moonlight.
Hudson thanked the landlord and went towards the exit with Miss Paddington. The housekeeper was still grinning.

! ÜBUNG 87

Übung 87: Ergänzen Sie die Sätze mit einem Pronomen!

1. "Is that *your* car over there, Elvira?"
2. "Do you want these books back?" "No, you can keep ______."
3. I like her. She's a good friend of ______.
4. Maria has just passed ______ driving test.
5. We could never part with ______ old car.
6. He told the children to do ______ homework.
7. Joe broke ______ arm playing football.

8. He told ______ that I was in danger.

9. “Do you know James?” “Yes, I work with ______.”

10. Oh no! I’ve left ______ umbrella on the bus!

Suddenly an old man stepped in front of them. His nose was red, and not only because of the wet, cold weather. The inspector could smell the alcohol on his breath. It was only politeness that stopped the inspector from turning his head away.

“You shouldn’t go to Thornwood’s castle, young fellow!” warned the old man, shaking his finger at Hudson. “Thornwood is very creepy. People say that he walks through the fog in this sort of weather, looking for victims whose blood he drinks.”

Hudson frowned and gently pushed the old man to one side.

“Thank you for your concern, sir. But I’m an inspector from Scotland Yard and I’m quite capable of taking care of myself and my assistant. Would you please let us pass?”

The old man nodded and looked at Miss Paddington. He took a small wooden cross out of his pocket. It looked as if he had carved it himself. Before Miss Paddington could react, he had pressed it into her hand.

“Here, take this,” said the old fellow. “You’ll need it. Be on your guard against old Thornwood! Be careful!”

The old man’s voice was still echoing through the fog when Inspector Hudson and Miss Paddington left the pub.

On the way back to the car Miss Paddington looked seriously at the little cross. The smile had left her face.

“I found the whole incident very amusing, James,” she said quietly. “But then that old man really sent a shiver down my spine.”

“Mine too, my dear Miss Paddington,” replied Hudson, and opened the door of the car. “Mine too …”

ÜBUNG 88 !

Übung 88: Entscheiden Sie, ob die folgenden Aussagen richtig sind! Markieren Sie: richtig ✓ falsch –

1. The pub-owner doesn't know the way to Thornwood's castle.
2. The other customers are listening to the conversation between Hudson and the pub-owner.
3. Miss Paddington was frightened when they went into the pub.
4. The old man thinks that Thornwood is dangerous.
5. The old man gives Miss Paddington something to protect her.
6. Hudson and Miss Paddington are laughing when they leave the pub.

Less than half an hour later, Inspector Hudson was driving the Bentley up the drive leading to Basil Thornwood's castle. The old walls really did look like something out of a horror film. The grey stones made the castle look so cool and uninviting that even the fog seemed to be keeping its distance. In contrast to the thick fog in the valley, up here only a few thin wisps dared to approach and shroud the battlements of the castle.

ÜBUNG 89 !

Übung 89: Unterstreichen Sie die richtige Alternative!

"Exactly the right sort of retirement home for a (1.) rented/retired vampire actor," murmured Miss Paddington, (2.) impressing/ impressed.

"It certainly is," agreed Hudson, "especially if this vampire actor now thinks he's a (3.) real/really vampire."

"Do you really believe that Basil Thornwood now (4.) absolutely/actually thinks he's a vampire?" asked Miss Paddington as

Hudson held the car door (5.) opened/open for her.
The inspector shook his head slowly.
"(6.) Either/Neither that – or Thornwood is cultivating an image in order to keep (7.) uninvited/uninviting visitors away. One way or another, he (8.) will/won't exactly be happy to see us."

"Well, I hope he doesn't go straight for our throats," replied Miss Paddington with a flash of black humour.
Inspector Hudson looked at his housekeeper with a serious expression on his face.
"Are you sure you want to come with me, Miss Paddington?" he asked. "I don't want to put you in unnecessary danger."
Instead of answering, Miss Paddington marched determinedly towards the large, wooden door of the castle.
"Come on, James!" she called. "This damp air isn't good for my rheumatism."
Hudson shook his head in admiration and walked up to the door with his housekeeper.
Of course the door did not have an electric doorbell, but instead there was a large doorknocker in the shape of a dragon's head.
The inspector grasped it and knocked three times on the wooden door.
The muffled bang had hardly died away when the mighty wooden door was opened as if by an invisible hand. A spooky creaking sound echoed through the fog.
Hudson swallowed.
For someone who didn't like visitors, Basil Thornwood was being surprisingly welcoming.
On the other hand, it was impossible to say what was waiting for them inside the old castle walls.

Übung 90: Füllen Sie die Lücken mit einem passenden Wort!
(bang, clap, creak, crash, hoot, pop, yell, squeak, thud, ticking)

1. The inspector heard the ____________ of a gun being fired.
2. There was a loud ____________ as she dropped all the plates.
3. If you listen carefully, you can hear the clock ____________.
4. The impatient motorists in the traffic jam began to _________ their horns.
5. I can hear a ____________. Your bike needs oiling.
6. She gave a ________ of terror as she fell through the trapdoor.
7. There was a __________ as he pulled the cork out of the bottle of champagne.
8. At the end of the concert the audience began to ____________.

"The door is probably opened by remote control," said James quietly, and cautiously stepped into the colossal entrance hall of the castle. Miss Paddington followed him.

There was nobody in the huge hall. The rough stone walls were decorated with old suits of armour and magnificent paintings. Hudson pointed to an enormous fireplace in which a fire was burning.

"Vampire or not," he said, "our Mr Thornwood seems to like being warm."

Miss Paddington was just about to reply when, all at once, the crackling fire in the fireplace went out.

Miss Paddington gasped. Hudson rushed over to the fireplace, which was as tall as a man. There was a slight smell of gas – similar to the smell that Miss Paddington's oven at home gave off when she was cooking.
"Don't worry, Miss Paddington," said Hudson in a soothing tone of voice. "The fire was only a gas flame. Also remote controlled. Our 'host' is trying to frighten us with a few tricks."

Übung 91: Finden Sie die weibliche Entsprechung für die männlichen Ausdrücke!

ÜBUNG 91 !

1. host __________
2. waiter __________
3. policeman __________
4. steward __________
5. actor __________
6. manager __________
7. husband __________
8. nephew __________
9. uncle __________
10. Mr __________

But Miss Paddington was looking round uncertainly.
"It's not that, James," she answered quietly. "It's this whole scenario – the door that opens by itself, the fire that suddenly goes out – I've seen it all before. In 'Encounter with a Vampire'. One of the

best films in which Basil Thornwood played the leading role. The only thing missing now is …"

Miss Paddington stopped speaking.

A madman's laugh echoed through the castle. It seemed to come from nowhere and everywhere at the same time.

"… a spooky laugh!"

Inspector Hudson pressed his housekeeper's arm reassuringly.

"How did 'Encounter with a Vampire' end, my dear?" he asked.

Miss Paddington gulped.

"Not well, James. The Count transformed all of his victims into vampires and with their help turned everyone in the region into slaves."

"Well, that's a pleasant prospect," replied the inspector, sarcastically. "I think it's time for us to change the script a little bit and take on the role of the director ourselves. Where was the Count hiding in this film, Miss Paddington?"

"Well, in the cellar under the castle, of course," answered Miss Paddington, somewhat nervously.

Inspector Hudson looked around. He was sure that they would find Basil Thornwood in the castle's cellar, too.

The only question was whether they were prepared for the 'Encounter with a Vampire'.

! ÜBUNG 92

Übung 92: Fügen Sie das passende Wort ein!

(comfortable, dangerous, discovered, mind, narrow, thoughts, tightly, tricks, underestimate)

Hudson noticed that Miss Paddington was holding the little wooden cross that the old man had given her 1. ____________ in her hand. He did not feel completely 2. ________________, either. Of course all this was just a collection of 3. ___________ rather than anything supernatural – and yet one should never 4. ___________ a madman.

By now Inspector Hudson was sure that Basil Thornwood had lost his 5. ___________. And a man who believed he was a vampire could be just as 6. ___________ as a real vampire.

Hudson pushed these unpleasant 7. ___________ out of his mind as he 8. ______________ a small door, behind which there was a 9. ___________ staircase.

With a movement of his hand he signalled to Miss Paddington that she should follow him.
The narrow stone steps led steeply downwards. Instead of electric lights there were small torches attached to the walls at regular intervals.
And once again their host demonstrated his love of drama.
As soon as Inspector Hudson and Miss Paddington passed one of the torches, it went out. This meant that the way downstairs was still illuminated while the way back disappeared into darkness.
"Just like in the film," whispered Miss Paddington.
Hudson nodded almost in admiration. Basil Thornwood had certainly gone to a lot of trouble to furnish his home authentically. The inspector asked himself what other surprises were waiting for him and Miss Paddington.
But wait – if the inside of the castle had been made to look like the film, then maybe Miss Paddington knew about possible traps.
Step by step, Hudson felt his way down the slippery stone stairs, glancing over his shoulder as he did so.

"Tell me, Miss Paddington, do you remember anything else about the film?"

The old lady was having difficulties keeping her balance on the narrow stairs. Despite this, she tried as hard as she could to remember some details of the film.

"I don't really know any more, James. After all, it's more than thirty years since I last saw 'Encounter with a Vampire'. I think there was something about a …"

"… trapdoor!" yelled Inspector Hudson, as the floor gave way under his feet and he was swallowed by the darkness.

Übung 93: Beantworten Sie die Fragen zum Text!

1. Who opened the door to the castle?

____

2. Where had Miss Paddington seen all of the tricks before?

____

3. Do Hudson and Miss Paddington feel comfortable in the castle?

____

4. What is used to light the staircase?

____

5. What happens to Hudson at the bottom of the staircase?

____

In the darkness it was impossible to tell how long the fall lasted or how deep Inspector Hudson and Miss Paddington fell into nothingness.

All they knew for sure was that the landing was fairly soft.

Basil Thornwood, undoubtedly the constructor of this trap, did not seem to want to injure his guests. At least not yet.

More shocked than really hurt, Hudson and his housekeeper landed on a few musty-smelling, but soft, cushions.

It took them a couple of seconds to get their bearings again, to be sure which way was up and which was down.

Hudson looked around. They were in a room which must have been extremely deep below the castle. It was probably part of an old secret passageway which the builders of the castle had constructed as an escape tunnel.

Übung 94: Unterstreichen Sie die richtige Alternative!

1. The tunnel was deeply/deep under the ground.
2. I have a highly/high opinion of her work.
3. He was driving very dangerously/dangerous on the slippery road.
4. It was raining heavily/heavy so we stayed at home.
5. She plays tennis very well/good. She always wins her matches.
6. He's a patiently/patient teacher. He doesn't mind explaining things several times.
7. Please be quietly/quiet. I'm trying to work.
8. Hudson stopped suddenly/sudden when he heard a noise.
9. He's angry/angrily with me because I crashed his car.
10. She's a well/good cook. Her food is always delicious!

Miss Paddington picked up a cushion and smelled it. With an expression of disgust she threw the rotting cushion over her shoulder.

"Yuck. I think our Mr Thornwood urgently needs a housekeeper."

Hudson heard a clicking sound.

He gulped.

"You can apply for the job personally, Miss Paddington – if we survive this little welcoming ceremony!"

The inspector pointed to the two long walls on the opposite sides of the room which had suddenly begun to move … towards each other!

"Oh my goodness!" exclaimed Miss Paddington. "Now he has really lost his mind! I've seen this death trap before! It's from 'Castle of a Thousand Deaths'! An Edgar Allan Poe film. A very free version of the original story, I might add!"

Hudson had jumped up and was trying to stop the walls from moving closer together.

Without success.

ÜBUNG 95 !

Übung 95: Unterstreichen Sie die nicht dazugehörigen acht Adjektive!

"Thank you for your boring film review, Miss Paddington, but first could you help me stop these beautiful walls somehow?"

Panting, Hudson and his hungry housekeeper braced themselves against the solid stone walls, which were being pressed together by a wonderful hidden mechanism.

The nice space between the two walls was now only a little more than a metre wide. But however hard the two interesting people tried, there didn't seem to be any way to stop the walls.

The lonely inspector and Miss Paddington were in a tight spot – in every sense of the word. Covered in sweat, Hudson pushed against the plastic wall with all of his strength.

"If we don't think of something in a minute," he panted, "we'll soon both be a lot thinner!"
"A diet that I wouldn't recommend to others," puffed Miss Paddington, "even if I ever have the chance to do so."
Suddenly, out of the blue, Miss Paddington knew how to save them. At least she hoped so!
The housekeeper reached into her handbag and took out the wooden cross that the old man had given her. She pressed it into the puzzled inspector's hand.
"Thank you, Miss Paddington," said Hudson, "But it's still a little too soon for my last prayer!"
"No!" shouted Miss Paddington. "Use it to block the wall! Quickly!"
Hudson could feel that the two walls were touching his chest and his back at the same time. Before it became too narrow, the inspector managed to get down on his knees and ram the wooden cross into the tiny gap between the moving wall and the stone floor.
The cross had the desired effect. Like a wedge it stuck fast under the wall and brought it to a grinding halt.
The hidden mechanism gave a screech of protest, then there was a cracking noise – and the walls stopped moving.

Übung 96: Welche Wörter gehören zusammen?

1. a terrifying	☐	of luck
2. a sigh	☐	of flowers
3. a good	☐	occasion
4. a narrow	☐	experience

5. a stroke	☐	rainfall
6. a happy	☐	of relief
7. a terrible	☐	of matches
8. a box	☐	idea
9. a heavy	☐	escape
10. a bunch	☐	headache

Hudson and Miss Paddington breathed a sigh of relief – as far as it was possible in the narrow space between the stone walls.

"That was a fantastic idea, Miss Paddington," exclaimed Hudson. "I would hug you if I had enough room."

The housekeeper beamed.

"Thank you very much, James. It was a sudden inspiration."

Then the old lady looked thoughtfully at the little wooden cross, which was still stuck between the wall and the floor.

"Who would have thought that that old man's cross really would save our lives?"

Hudson nodded.

"It really was fate. We owe the man a couple of drinks – but first we have to catch Basil Thornwood … after we've freed ourselves from this trap."

Hudson and Miss Paddington began to look for an exit. After a little while they found a small door which led from the corridor of death into another room.

This door was so well-hidden in the wall of the corridor that it could only be found after a long, careful search, a search that took longer than it would have taken the stone walls to complete their deadly work.

Inspector Hudson and Miss Paddington looked around.

They were standing in a huge underground cellar that was lit by torches. In the four corners of the room there were life-sized stone

statues, which seemed to be watching them with cold eyes.
But it was something else altogether that made Inspector Hudson's and Miss Paddington's blood run cold:
A black, shining coffin was lying on a stone platform in the middle of the cellar.
And the lid was opening slowly.

Übung 97: Vervollständigen Sie die Aussagen!

1. When Hudson and Miss Paddington fell through the trapdoor ______________.
   a) ☐ they hurt themselves badly
   b) ☐ they landed on an old sofa
   c) ☐ they landed on something soft

2. The moving walls ______________.
   a) ☐ came towards them very quickly
   b) ☐ were too heavy to push apart
   c) ☐ were an idea from one of Thornwood's films

3. Hudson stopped the walls from moving ______________.
   a) ☐ when it was too late
   b) ☐ before Miss Paddington had an idea
   c) ☐ just in time

4. The underground cellar ______________.
   a) ☐ seemed to be Thornwood's hiding place
   b) ☐ was completely dark
   c) ☐ was very cold and wet

5. A shining coffin was lying ________________.

a) ☐ in the middle of the cellar

b) ☐ in a middle of a cellar

c) ☐ in the middle in our cellar

A gaunt, skinny figure rose from the coffin.
Instinctively Inspector Hudson and Miss Paddington took a step back.
"Th-the Count," stammered Miss Paddington in horror, although of course she knew exactly who it really was there in front of her.
"Mr Basil Thornwood," said Inspector Hudson, taking out his police badge, "I'm arresting you for the mean robbery of a security van!"
A deep, echoing laugh came from the mouth of the vampire. The old man's eyes glittered with insanity.
And two long, yellow fangs flashed in the light of the torches.
With astonishing agility for someone his age, the evil actor swung himself out of his coffin. His long black cape fluttered behind him.
"Basil Thornwood is dead," laughed the vampire. "I am now … Count Dracula!"

ÜBUNG 98 !

Übung 98: Bringen Sie die Wörter in die richtige Reihenfolge!

1. obviously The mad was man completely old

____

2. were spoke They the shocked vampire when

____

3. actor to Hudson the arrest old wanted

---

4. huge laugh the A echoed hall loud through

---

5. fit the It man was how amazing was

---

6. long cape The fluttered around

"But, more importantly, you're mad," replied the inspector in a firm voice. "And you're a criminal!"

Thornwood laughed again. Then, with incredible self-confidence, he walked towards Hudson and Miss Paddington.

"Yes, it's true. I robbed that security van. Times have changed. Nowadays even a count of noble blood needs money to get even with the sinners!"

"The sinners?" asked Hudson with a frown. "Who do you mean by that?"

Thornwood came a step closer.

"Who do I mean by that? Those jumped-up film people who misused my name for their cheap rubbish, that's *who*! Just imagine, that Ratcliff even had the nerve to offer me a guest appearance in his trashy film. A *guest appearance*! There's only one true Count Dracula … and that's me! And soon he will also be one of my slaves!"

With these words, Thornwood took a step forwards and threw himself at Inspector Hudson.

ÜBUNG 99 !

Übung 99: Vervollständigen Sie die Sätze mit einem Körperteil!
(arms, eye, feet, foot, mouth, nerve, nose, skin and bones)

1. He's got a __________________ coming back here after all the trouble he caused!
2. I've been really busy all day – absolutely rushed off my __________________.
3. When he was skiing last year, he broke his left ____________.
4. Stop sticking your __________________ into my business! It's nothing to do with you!
5. I saw the boys stealing the sweets but I turned a blind ______ ____________. I didn't say anything.
6. She's really thin. She's all ____________________________.
7. She's really friendly. We'd never met before but she welcomed me with open __________________.
8. Tom's got such a big __________________. He told everyone my secret!

Miss Paddington screamed in horror and dropped her handbag. The housekeeper was paralysed with shock.
The vampire took Hudson completely by surprise with his attack, making him lose his balance. The inspector fell backwards and crashed onto the hard stone floor.
The old actor lay on top of Hudson with all of his weight and pressed the inspector to the floor.

Übung 100: Unterstreichen Sie die Gegenteile im Text!
(1. sanity 2. weakness 3. pull 4. sweet-smelling 5. powerful 6. blunt 7. harmless)

Madness seemed to have given the man unbelievable strength. Inspector Hudson tried to push Thornwood off him, but the actor had him firmly in his grasp.
Foul breath hit the inspector in the face when Thornwood opened his mouth, showing his fangs. Hudson felt helpless.
With a horrible, ear-splitting laugh, Thornwood opened his jaw even wider. The sharp, yellowish fangs were only centimetres from Hudson's neck.
It seemed that the insane actor really did intend to bite the inspector! And, vampire or no vampire, he could give Hudson a fatal injury with those false fangs!

The inspector thought feverishly. The fangs were only millimetres away from the main blood vessel in his neck.
Out of the corner of his eye he noticed Miss Paddington's handbag lying next to him on the floor.
Miss Paddington had already used it to stop one false vampire today – maybe it would work a second time. Hudson remembered what Miss Paddington had taken out of her handbag in Sir Reginald's office that morning.
The inspector stretched out his arm and felt inside the handbag with the tips of his fingers. As soon as he felt something soft, he grabbed it and pulled it out.
The garlic sausage sandwich!
Thornwood snapped at the inspector's throat.
Hudson stuffed the sandwich into the madman's mouth.

Basil Thornwood opened his eyes wide in surprise. Then he gasped for breath and let go of the inspector.

A terrible scream came from the mouth of the would-be vampire. Choking, he tried to spit out the bread and the garlic sausage.

Thornwood jumped up and staggered through the cellar towards his coffin. His white face had become even more pale.

Panting, Thornwood held his throat, and collapsed, unconscious, a few steps away from his coffin.

! *Übung 101: Welches Wort ist das "schwarze Schaf"?*

1. garlic, carrot, cucumber, fruit ____________
2. sausage, eggs, ham, bacon ____________
3. breakfast, lunch, menu, dinner ____________
4. plate, cup, saucer, frying pan ____________
5. butter, sandwich, toast, loaf ____________
6. bake, roast, slice, fry ____________
7. tin, saucepan, jar, tube ____________
8. cut, munch, chew, lick ____________
9. cheese, yoghurt, butter, honey ____________
10. starter, main course, steak, dessert ____________

Inspector Hudson and Miss Paddington watched the macabre show, holding their breath.

Gradually the housekeeper came back to life.

Hudson knelt down next to the actor and felt for his pulse.
"He's only unconscious," said the inspector, relieved.
Miss Paddington came closer.

Übung 102: Welche Präposition gehört wohin?

1. interested	☐	on
2. surprised	☐	to
3. look forward	☐	at
4. keen	☐	in
5. consist	☐	of

"But how was that possible? He's not really a vampire, after all! Why did he react so strongly to the garlic?"
Hudson shrugged his shoulders.
"I suppose he simply identified so closely with his role that he really believed that garlic is poisonous to him. The effect was the same as it would have been for a real vampire."
Miss Paddington nodded thoughtfully.
"So it was actually his own madness that was his downfall …"
"That's right," agreed the inspector. "His madness and your sandwiches."
"Not a very good recommendation for my cooking," said Miss Paddington with a frown.
"Don't worry," grinned the inspector. "I won't tell anyone. And now let's find the way out of this cellar."
Three months later.
Bent down low, Inspector Hudson ran across the fog-covered cemetery. A spooky laugh could be heard.
Hudson spun around.

A dark figure in a long, black cape rose up behind him. Vampire teeth glinted in the moonlight.

The vampire threw himself at the inspector.

Hudson cleverly avoided his attacker and kicked him with a skilful karate kick.

The vampire groaned and was thrown a couple of metres backwards.

Inspector Hudson reached into his jacket pocket and took out a strangely shaped pistol.

"Go to hell, *sucker*!" shouted Hudson, and pulled the trigger. A salvo of tiny wooden stakes shot out of the gun. The wooden bullets hit the vampire, who turned to dust with a terrible scream.

! ÜBUNG 103

Übung 103: Welche Aktivität passt zu welchem Objekt?

1. shoot	☐ a course
2. cut	☐ a present
3. tie	☐ someone to a party
4. wrap	☐ a table clean
5. take	☐ a gun
6. attend	☐ coffee
7. invite	☐ with scissors
8. wish	☐ something up with strings
9. wipe	☐ a photo
10. stir	☐ someone luck

At the same moment, the light flickered on in the little cinema.

Ray Ratcliff, the director, looked at Hudson expectantly.

"Well, what do you think, inspector? When I read in the newspaper about how your case ended I rewrote the whole script. I hope you are happy with the actor who's playing the role of Hudson. What you've just seen is only a rough cut, of course. In the final version there will be hot techno music playing throughout the whole scene."

"Well, I enjoyed it," said Miss Paddington, who was sitting next to Hudson. "I could get used to this new kind of horror film. Although I must say that I don't need any more scary adventures for the time being."

Übung 104: Sind folgende Aussagen richtig?
Markieren Sie: richtig ✓ falsch –

ÜBUNG 104 !

1. Hudson starred in a horror film.
2. Ratcliff got an idea for his film from Hudson's vampire case.
3. They have just watched the final version of the film.
4. Miss Paddington thought the film was good.
5. Miss Paddington is ready for another adventure.

Elvira Elliot was sitting on the other side of the inspector and patted him proudly on the shoulder. Her injured leg was now completely healed.

"You're going to be a star, James. The media will be fighting to get an interview with you. Everyone will want to hear the real story behind 'Dracula 2003'. When I arrived there were already a few reporters standing in front of the film studio …"

Inspector Hudson sighed and rubbed his forehead.

They say that Canada is very nice at this time of year, he thought. And, best of all, it's far, far away …

THE END

Abschlusstest

Übung 1: Finden Sie die Synonyme und setzen Sie die richtige Ziffer ein!

1. start	☐	observe
2. strong	☐	depressed
3. unhappy	☐	powerful
4. escape	☐	delighted
5. hurry	☐	begin
6. watch	☐	rush
7. pleased	☐	run away

Übung 2: Vervollständigen Sie die Sätze!

1. She stole all my money. She is a ________.
2. Thornwood lived in an old ________ in the country.
3. They sell all sorts of different things at a ________ ________.
4. Vampires drink ________.
5. A ________ is a big group of people who have come together in one place.
6. She was wearing a lot of ______ - ______ : lipstick, eyeshadow and face powder.
7. An ______________ collects injured people and takes them to hospital.
8. An ________________ sees an accident or a crime take place.

9. A _____________ writes articles for a newspaper.

10. A _____________ is a boat that goes under the water.

Übung 3: Was gehört zusammen? Setzen Sie die richtige Ziffer ein!

1. take	☐	a holiday
2. fill in	☐	someone a favour
3. throw	☐	a car
4. catch	☐	shopping
5. do	☐	one's time
6. remind	☐	a letter
7. boil	☐	a ball
8. go	☐	a form
9. lend	☐	a cold
10. book	☐	water
11. rent	☐	someone some money
12. receive	☐	someone to do something

Übung 4: Welcher Satz enthält die richtige Übersetzung?

1. Wo ist die nächste Bank, bitte?
   a) ☐ Where is the next bank, please?
   b) ☐ Where is the nearest bank, please?

2. Er kontrollierte mein Handgepäck.
   a) ☐ He checked my hand luggage.
   b) ☐ He controlled my hand luggage.

3. Ich wohne hier seit zehn Jahren.
   a) ☐ I live here since ten years.
   b) ☐ I have lived here for ten years.

4. Was meinst du? Soll ich die Jacke kaufen?
   a) ☐ What do you mean? Shall I buy the jacket?
   b) ☐ What do you think? Shall I buy the jacket?

5. Abends höre ich gerne Musik.
   a) ☐ I like listening to music in the evenings.
   b) ☐ I like hearing music in the evenings.

Übung 5: Welches Wort ist das „schwarze Schaf"?

1. kitchen, stairs, bedroom, bathroom ______________
2. cat, dog, goldfish, pet ______________
3. lion, wood, forest, trees ______________
4. pavement, zebra crossing, bus, traffic lights ______________
5. talk, speak, chat, cry ______________
6. trousers, shoes, scissors, glasses ______________
7. cat, mouse, screen, keyboard ______________

Übung 6: Unterstreichen Sie die richtige Alternative!

1. Please remember/remind me to phone her this evening.
2. The internet provides the most up-to-date/actual information.

3. He's a colleague of me/mine.
4. I don't like tea and I don't like coffee, either/too.
5. He was very angry and he cried/shouted at the children.
6. They love going for walks in the countryside/nature.
7. If she isn't careful, she'll lose/loose her job.
8. There's too less/little time to do the work properly.

Übung 7: Welche Gegenteile gehören zusammen? Setzen Sie die richtige Ziffer ein!

1. arrival	☐ pessimistic
2. high	☐ follow
3. cellar	☐ departure
4. dawn	☐ similar
5. optimistic	☐ dusk
6. different	☐ low
7. lead	☐ roof

Übung 8: Was bedeuten folgende Redewendungen?

1. Miss Paddington has a heart of gold.
   a) ☐ She's a very kind, generous person.
   b) ☐ She has a lot of money.
   c) ☐ She has problems with her heart.

2. Andy let the cat out of the bag.
   a) ☐ He allowed the cat to run away.
   b) ☐ He told people a secret when he shouldn't have.
   c) ☐ He told a good joke.

Übung 9: Wie heißen die Obst- und Gemüsesorten richtig!

1. plpae ____________________
2. cehryr ____________________
3. cumbcuerb ____________________
4. nabana ____________________
5. otomta ____________________
6. cehap ____________________
7. mizae ____________________
8. elonm ____________________
9. rreybswatr ____________________
8. elonm ____________________
9. rreybswatr ____________________
10. engroa ____________________
11. neab ____________________

Übung 10: Welchem Beruf gehen die Menschen nach, die in diesen Institutionen arbeiten?

1. hospital	☐ waiter
2. ranch	☐ priest
3. restaurant	☐ doctor
4. school	☐ captain
5. church	☐ farmer
6. ship	☐ teacher

Lösungen

Übung 1: 1. midnight/midday 2. light/heavy 3. big/small 4. tall/short 5. beautiful/ugly 6. dark/light 7. evening/morning 8. thick/thin 9. clean/dirty 10. happy/sad
Übung 2: 1. b 2. a 3. a 4. b
Übung 3: 2. man 3. rose 4. hands 5. air 6. moonlight 7. pub 8. walk 9. night 10. park
Übung 4: 1. white 2. red 3. black 4. green 5. brown 6. grey 7. yellow 8. blue 9. Orange
Übung 5: 1. fish and chips 2. bread and butter 3. salt and pepper 4. night and day 5. black and white 6. up and down 7. brush and comb 8. husband and wife 9. brother and sister 10. son and daughter 11. work and play 12. fruit and vegetables 13. sun and rain 14. summer and winter 15. now and again
Übung 6: 2. inspector 3. pair 4. trousers 5. road worker 6. waistcoat 7. head 8. fashion
Übung 7: 1. cap 2. slippers 3. trousers 4. skirt 5. shorts 6. dress 7. shirt
Lösung: clothes
Übung 8: 1. tired 2. shocked 3. hate 4. driver 5. policeman 6. bank 7. busy 8. angry 9. glass
Übung 9: CDs, furniture, lamps, computer systems, fax machines
Übung 10: 1. clown 2. actor 3. juggler 4. fire-eater 5. mime artist 6. street entertainer 7. acrobat 8. animal trainer
Übung 11: 2. I'm afraid that the tourists will stay away. 3. It was a very good idea. 4. Let's stop and watch the mime artist. 5. A lot of tourists go to that restaurant.
Übung 12: 1. sighed 2. midday 3. narrow 4. Crowds 5. stopped 6. prices 7. difficult 8. easy 9. checked 10. wallet
Übung 13: 1. Yes, there were a lot of people at the market. 2. No, nobody stole it. 3. They were watching a mime artist. 4. Yes, he was very good. 5. Because the mime artist pretended to slip on a banana skin.
Übung 14: 1. for 2. out 3. towards 4. to 5. at 6. towards 7. off 8. at
Übung 15: 1. talk 2. park 3. cry 4. stylist 5. water 6. sweating 7. slow 8. throw 9. watch 10. ship
Übung 16: 1. richtig 2. richtig 3. falsch 4. richtig 5. falsch
Übung 17: 1. Hudson and Elvira were very surprised. 2. The man was riding a small bicycle. 3. The artist could not escape. 4. His friends tried to help him. 5. They ran very fast.
Übung 18: 1. thin 2. quickly 3. high 4. heavy 5. loud 6. late 7. ugly 8. young
Übung 19: 1. foot 2. chin 3. knee 4. gum 5. ear 6. eyebrow 7. ankle 8. stomach 9. lip 10. shoulder
Lösung: fingernail
Übung 20: 1. finger print 2. bus stop 3. alarm clock 4. phone call 5. washing machine 6. car park 7. sunglasses 8. mobile phone 9. sign post 10. traffic lights

Übung 21: 1. a 2. c 3. c 4. b 5. a
Übung 22: 2. hotel 3. station 4. post office 5. supermarket 6. theatre 7. restaurant 8. cinema 9. museum 10. town hall
Übung 23: 1. She went to the bathroom. 2. The woman took a shower. 3. All he wanted was to go home and go to bed. 4. Suddenly she turned around starting to sing a christmas song. 5. I live just around the corner.
Übung 24: 1. open/closed 2. interesting/boring 3. dangerous/harmless 4. pleasant/unpleasant 5. empty/full 6. high/low 7. lazy/hard-working 8. polite/rude 9. healthy/ill 10. nice/horrible
Übung 25: 1. Elvira asked her friends to come in. 2. They wondered what the noise could be. 3. She broke her leg and had to stay in bed. 4. Could you put these flowers in some water? 5. It is boring in hospital if you have nothing to do.
Übung 26: 1. cupboard 2. suddenly 3. boss 4. why 5. tie 6. pretty 7. astonishment 8. schoolgirl 9. knock 10. nurses
Übung 27: 1. say hello 2. watch television 3. pay a bill 4. make a phone call 5. give a present 6. read a book 7. brush one's teeth 8. do some work 9. drive a car 10. ride a bike
Übung 28: 1. b 2. b 3. a 4. b 5. a
Übung 29: 1. No, she doesn't. 2. He was hiding from the nurses. 3. He brought her some flowers. 4. She gave Elvira some detective stories. 5. Yes, he does.
Übung 30: 1. politics 2. sports 3. business 4. travel 5. current affairs 6. arts 7. education
Übung 31: figure, victims, person, madman, couple, stranger, villain, police, someone
Übung 32: 1. film 2. head 3. magazine 4. eyewitness 5. fat 6. hospital 7. healthy 8. relaxed 9. terrible 10. lift
Übung 33: 1. a 2. b 3. b 4. a 5. c
Übung 34: 1. elevator/lift 2. sketch/drawing 3. smile/grin 4. nonsense/rubbish 5. way out/exit 6. hurry/rush 7. wallet/purse 8. notice/catch sight of 9. discuss/talk about 10. surprise/astonishment
Übung 35: 1. home 2. policemen 3. room 4. pot of tea 5. housekeeper 6. steaming 7. cup 8. town
Übung 36: 1. plant 2. armchair 3. television 4. cushion 5. curtain 6. board games 7. carpet 8. bookcase 9. remote control 10. lamp Lösung: living room
Übung 37: 1. famous actor 2. horror movie 3. friendly smile 4. dangerous criminal 5. comfortable chair 6. good news 7. bright light 8. thick fog 9. close friend 10. fast car
Übung 38: 1. into 2. Half an hour ago 3. in front of 4. for 5. wife 6. every evening 7. change 8. bought 9. paid for 10. cheap
Übung 39: 1. c 2. b 3. b 4. b 5. a
Übung 40: 1. Where 2. Who 3. What 4. When 5. How 6. Why 7. Which 8. What 9. Who 10. Where

Übung 41: anser (answer), lorghter (laughter), theirselfes (themselves), breethed (breathed), closser (closer), lite (light), court (caught), waring (wearing), wurst (worst), sranger's (stranger's)
Übung 42: 1. up 2. in 3. off 4. on 5. down 6. up 7. off 8. up 9. down 10. in
Übung 43: 1. telephone 2. sleep 3. vampire 4. kill 5. eyes 6. radio 7. clock 8. week
Übung 44: 1. dishonest 2. lucky 3. impatient 4. generous 5. stupid 6. foreign 7. thirsty 8. careful 9. shy 10. reliable
Übung 45: 1. There's nothing better than a nice cup of tea. 2. Hudson asked his housekeeper to help him. 3. Why does a vampire need to steal money? 4. Could you come into the office right away? 5. He put on his new blue suit and a tie.
Übung 46: 1. car and petrol 2. tea and sugar 3. shoes and socks 4. knife and fork 5. table and chair 6. computer and printer 7. airport and plane 8. cinema and film 9. theatre and play 10. bank and money
Übung 47: 1. Nobody 2. bankrupt 3. earned 4. lonely 5. life 6. years 7. strange 8. story 9. at night 10. traffic lights
Übung 48: 1. take 2. do 3. make 4. do 5. make 6. Take 7. make 8. make 9. do 10. take
Übung 49: 1. young 2. tall 3. long 4. sharp 5. crazy 6. angry 7. serious 8. sensational 9. frightened 10. surprised
Übung 50: 1. garlic 2. banana 3. onion 4. butter 5. grapes 6. lemon 7. raspberry 8. potato 9. honey 10. ice-cream
Übung 51: 1. He is an actor who played Dracula in the 1970s. 2. No, he doesn't. 3. He lives in a lonely house in the country. 4. No, there aren't. 5. No, they opened again last year. 6. He decides to go to Anvil Studios.
Übung 52: 1. entrance/exit 2. enormous/tiny 3. allowed/forbidden 4. famous/unknown 5. early/late 6. ceiling/floor 7. lazy/hard-working 8. formal/casual 9. unusual/ordinary 10. stop/start
Übung 53: 1. apart from 2. excellent 3. series 4. sale 5. shook 6. part with 7. What a pity 8. goodbye 9. Just a moment 10. made
Übung 54: 1. long 2. possibly 3. arrive 4. helpless 5. choke 6. shout 7. ordinary 8. gasp 9. grin 10. behind
Übung 55: 1. make a film 2. ask a question 3. knock on/at the door 4. solve a problem 5. wear clothes 6. tell a lie 7. deliver a message 8. smoke a pipe 9. pass a test 10. commit a crime
Übung 56: 1. b 2. b 3. a 4. a 5. b
Übung 57: 1. Not many people are swimming in the lake. 2. He works in a hospital. 3. She went to be early. 4. I work as a gardener. 5. Be careful of the sharks.
Übung 58: 1. is 2. does 3. Are 4. did 5. Am 6. do 7. are 8. were 9. Was 10. did
Übung 59: 1. director 2. assistant 3. housekeeper 4. policeman 5. cameraman 6. porter 7. gardener 8. manager 9. vampire
Übung 60: 1. falsch 2. richtig 3. richtig 4. falsch 5. falsch 6. richtig

Übung 61: 1. didn't have a clue 2. key 3. playing the role 4. fantastic 5. imagine 6. cautious 7. idea 8. coach
Übung 62: 1. an 2. – 3. the/the 4. a 5. – 6. a 7. the/the 8. The 9. a 10. a
Übung 63: 1. Miss Paddington could not believe her eyes. 2. The actor pushed the inspector to the floor. 3. The director knew something about the vampire attacks. 4. I'd like to ask you a few questions. 5. Could you tell me where you were last night?
Übung 64: 1. surprising 2. surprised 3. interesting 4. exciting 5. tired 6. tiring 7. boring/interesting 8. excited 9. shocked 10. disappointing
Übung 65: 1. moon 2. earth 3. mountains 4. space 5. helmet 6. everyone 7. recording 8. baseball 9. hair 10. dust
Übung 66: 1. furious 2. moustache 3. destroy 4. apologise 5. earth 6. sky 7. library 8. post office 9. studio
Übung 67: buildings, billboards, neon signs, street lamp, dustbins, signpost, mail box, newspaper stand, taxi
Übung 68: 1. on 2. in 3. at 4. in 5. at 6. in 7. at/on 8. in 9. at 10. at
Übung 69: brige (bridge), wals (walls), live (life), roome (room), quitely (quietly), throow (through), eazy (easy), evry (every), nobodie (nobody)
Übung 70: 1. c 2. e 3. g 4. a 5. h 6. i 7. j 8. b 9. f 10. d
Übung 71: 1. It was about a submarine. 2. Yes, it did. 3. No, he was very quiet. 4. In a torpedo tube. 5. She hit him with her handbag.
Übung 72: 1. prison/jail 2. taxi/cab 3. lift/elevator 4. pavement/sidewalk 5. rubbish/garbage 6. petrol/gasoline 7. lorry/truck 8. motorway/freeway 9. holiday/vacation 10. flat/apartment
Übung 73: 1. what about 2. afford 3. have 4. shouldn't 5. sorrowfully 6. lose 7. his shoulders 8. nothing 9. Unless 10. pricked up
Übung 74: 1. mess 2. fun 3. bedroom 4. comfortable 5. plate 6. screen 7. kitchen 8. fascinate 9. freeze Lösung: submarine
Übung 75: 1. bathroom 2. pub 3. garage 4. cemetery 5. camping site 6. stadium 7. beach 8. forest 9. mountain 10. border
Übung 76: 1. b 2. c 3. b 4. a 5. a
Übung 77: 1. were 2. began 3. gave 4. left 5. went 6. was 7. smiled 8. lost 9. thought 10. came
Übung 78: 1. b 2. a 3. a 4. b
Übung 79: 1. laptop 2. printer 3. mobile 4. keyboard 5. modem 6. Internet 7. mouse 8. e-mail
Übung 80: 1. head 2. scream 3. everything 4. hide 5. blanket 6. quickly 7. patients 8. read 9. volume 10. cinema
Übung 81: 1. find out/discover 2. freeze/turn to ice 3. biography/life story 4. most famous/best known 5. switch off/turn off 6. close/shut 7. fan/admirer

8. scream/shriek 9. position/place 10. keen/eager
Übung 82: 1. He owes me some money. 2. My mobile phone rang and I answered it. 3. Take the money and put it in your pocket! 4. It's not worth waiting any longer. 5. We must find out about Basil Thornwood.
Übung 83: 1. in his heyday 2. over 3. for ages 4. retired from the public eye 5. make a comeback 6. wasn't successful 7. regretfully 8. nowadays
Übung 84: 1. attack/defend 2. country/city 3. question/answer 4. simple/complicated 5. public/private 6. alive/dead 7. past/future 8. hide/reveal 9. artificial/natural 10. brave/cowardly
Übung 85: 1. park a car 2. find the way 3. spend money 4. pour a drink 5. listen to the radio 6. hear a noise 7. make an appointment 8. dig a hole 9. remember someone's birthday 10. sign a letter
Übung 86: 1. outside 2. cigarette 3. clouds 4. customers 5. walked 6. followed 7. Excuse 8. afraid
Übung 87: 1. your 2. them 3. mine 4. her 5. our 6. their 7. his 8. me 9. him 10. my
Übung 88: 1. falsch 2. richtig 3. falsch 4. richtig 5. richtig 6. falsch
Übung 89: 1. retired 2. impressed 3. real 4. actually 5. open 6. Either 7. uninvited 8. won't
Übung 90: 1. bang 2. crash 3. ticking 4. hoot 5. squeak 6. yell 7. pop 8. clap
Übung 91: 1. hostess 2. waitress 3. policewoman 4. stewardess 5. actress 6. manageress 7. wife 8. niece 9. aunt 10. Mrs/Miss/Ms
Übung 92: 1. tightly 2. comfortable 3. tricks 4. underestimate 5. mind 6. dangerous 7. thoughts 8. discovered 9. narrow
Übung 93: 1. Basil Thornwood, by remote control. 2. In a film called 'Encounter with a Vampire'. 3. No, they don't. 4. There are small torches on the wall. 5. He falls through a trapdoor.
Übung 94: 1. deep 2. high 3. dangerously 4. heavily 5. well 6. patient 7. quiet 8. suddenly 9. angry 10. good
Übung 95: boring, beautiful, hungry, wonderful, nice, interesting, lonely, plastic
Übung 96: 1. a terrifying experience 2. a sigh of relief 3. a good idea 4. a narrow escape 5. a stroke of luck 6. a happy occasion 7. a terrible headache 8. a box of matches 9. a heavy rainfall 10. a bunch of flowers
Übung 97: 1. c 2. b 3. c 4. a 5. a
Übung 98: 1. The old man was obviously completely mad. 2. They were shocked when the vampire spoke. 3. Hudson wanted to arrest the old actor. 4. A loud laugh echoed through the huge hall. 5. It was amazing how fit the man was 6. The long cape fluttered around.
Übung 99: 1. nerve 2. feet 3. foot 4. nose 5. eye 6. skin and bones 7. arms 8. mouth
Übung 100: 1. madness 2. strength 3. push 4. foul 5. helpless 6. sharp 7. fatal
Übung 101: 1. fruit 2. eggs 3. menu 4. frying pan 5. butter 6. slice 7. saucepan

8. cut 9. honey 10. steak
Übung 102: 1. interested in 2. surprised at 3. look forward to 4. keen on 5. consist of
Übung 103: 1. shoot a gun 2. cut with scissors 3. tie something up with strings 4. wrap a present 5. take a photo 6. attend a course 7. invite someone to a party 8. wish someone luck 9. wipe a table clean 10. stir coffee
Übung 104: 1. falsch 2. richtig 3. falsch 4. richtig 5. falsch

Lösungen Abschlusstest

Übung 1: 1. start/begin 2. strong/powerful 3. unhappy/depressed 4. escape/run away 5. hurry/rush 6. watch/observe 7. pleased/delighted
Übung 2: 1. thief 2. castle 3. flea market 4. blood 5. crowd 6. make-up 7. ambulance 8. eye witness 9. journalist 10. submarine
Übung 3: 1. take one's time 2. fill in a form 3. throw a ball 4. catch a cold 5. do someone a favour 6. remind someone to do something 7. boil water 8. go shopping 9. lend someone some money 10. book a holiday 11. rent a car 12. receive a letter
Übung 4: 1. b 2. a 3. a 4. b 5. a
Übung 5: 1. stairs 2. pet 3. lion 4. bus 5. cry 6. scissors 7. cat
Übung 6: 1. remind 2. up-to-date 3. mine 4. either 5. shouted 6. countryside 7. lose 8. little
Übung 7: 1. arrival/departure 2. high/low 3. cellar/roof 4. dawn/dusk 5. optimistic/pessimistic 6. different/similar 7. lead/follow
Übung 8: 1. a 2. b
Übung 9: 1. apple 2. cherry 3. cucumber 4. banana 5. tomato 6. peach 7. maize 8. melon 9. strawberry 10. orange 11. bean
Übung 10: 1. doctor 2. farmer 3. waiter 4. teacher 5. priest 6. captain